When the Pieces Don't Fit
God Makes the Difference

Glaphré

Foreword by Gloria Gaither

Zondervan Publishing House
Grand Rapids, Michigan

Requests for information should be addressed to:
Zondervan Publishing House
Grand Rapids, Michigan 49530

WHEN THE PIECES DON'T FIT: GOD MAKES THE DIFFERENCE
Copyright © 1984 by Glaphré Gilliland

·Library of Congress Cataloging in Publication Data
Gilliland, Glaphré.
    When the pieces don't fit.
    1. Christian life—1960– . 2. God. 3. Gilliland, Glaphré. I. Title.
BV4501.2.G51127 1984   248.4   84-16807
ISBN 0-310-45341-0

Scripture references used in this book are indicated as follows:

LB: Verses marked LB are taken from *The Living Bible*. Copyright © 1971 by
Tyndale House Publishers, Wheaton, Illinois. Used by permission.
NEB: From *The New English Bible*. Copyright © The Delegates of the Oxford
University Press and the Syndics of the Cambridge University Press, 1961, 1970.
Reprinted by permission.
NIV: HOLY BIBLE New International Version (North American Edition),
copyright © 1978, The International Bible Society. Used by permission.
RSV: Biblical quotations marked RSV are from the *Revised Standard Version* of the
Bible copyrighted 1946, 1952, © 1971, 1973. Used by permission.
KJV: Verses marked KJV are taken from the *King James Version* of the Bible.
JB: From the *Jerusalem Bible*.

Edited by Anne Severance
Designed by Ann Cherryman

Printed in the United States of America

92 93 94 / DP / 17 16 15 14

To my parents
Ponder and Floy Gilliland

for being exactly
what God had in mind
when He created parents

*M*y special thanks to:

my Prayer Partners who diligently prayed for me as I wrote, and prayed for you who would read this book.

the people who invested in *you* by giving me permission to share their stories.

Anne Severance, for more than sensitive and skillful editing—for praying and caring; the staff of Zondervan Publishing House, for a mutual commitment to God which translates into their work.

Lois Bock, for being God's door opener for this book—as with so many things in my life; Barbara Daniels, for supportive friendship, typing my scribbling through many drafts, and encouraging each step; Doris Littrell, for generously giving needed input to a novice writer.

my family: Dad and Mom, Ron and Lin, Sheri, Marsha, Christa and Cara. For believing in this message. In this book. In me.

God. For Freedom. For Wholeness. For Making a Difference!

Contents

Foreword

*L*ofty words, pious repetitions,
   Phrases great and grand
     Are not what He demands.
Open hands are more
     than just a gesture:
   I bring all of me
   And He brings all of Him.
Sweet communion!
I hardly know
     where He stops
     and I begin.
Sweet Freedom!
   There's no price too high;
   It's been worth it all to know
     I'm clean within!
I will praise Him,
   Knowing that my praise will cost me
     EVERYTHING!
I will praise Him,
   Praise Him with the joy
     that comes from knowing
       that I have held back nothing.
   And *He is* Lord.
    He is Lord!
     He is Lord!*

*Lyrics by Gloria Gaither. Music by John W. Thompson. © Copyright 1978 by William J. Gaither (ASCAP) and Paragon Music Corp. (ASCAP) International copyright secured.

A few years ago I wrote those words and hoped I knew what they meant. I did know that prayer wasn't just an incantation and that praise wasn't just a noise we make. But to count the cost of making Jesus truly Lord and making prayer a way of life was a commitment I was only beginning to learn how to make. I am still only learning how to really *live* my prayer and praise.

Glaphré *knows* what it means to live like that. Her praise *walks* and her prayers *serve*. She knows what it means to give praise that "costs her everything." And she has also experienced the joy that only comes from "knowing that she has held back nothing, and He is Lord!"

To those of us who have ever said, "Lord, teach me to pray," God sends Glaphré. And she teaches us anew what our Lord taught: to pray simply, to pray directly, to pray with the mind of Christ, and to pray ceaselessly. She teaches by showing us how to take the total risk of living as Jesus commands.

What a gift she has been to my life! What a gift this book is to us all! My prayer is that all of you who read this book will find in it the inspiration to risk the great adventure of becoming first-name friends with the Creator of the universe. May you learn to talk to Him as naturally as you breathe, and to follow Him as naturally as you walk.

Part 1.

God Makes the Difference In Our Plans

WE EXAMINE OUR LIVES,
EMBRACE OUR DESIRES,
AND CREATE OUR PLANS.

EAGERLY,
WE ENTRUST OUR FRESH DESIGN
TO GOD.

WE'RE SURE ... WE KNOW ...
THIS PLAN WILL MAKE THE DIFFERENCE!
THIS PLAN WILL ENSURE OUR HAPPINESS,
OUR FULFILLMENT.

SINCE OUR BLUEPRINT IS SO CLEAR
WHY WON'T GOD COOPERATE?

Chapter 1.

Rushing Ahead

They did not bother to ask the Lord,
but went ahead (Josh. 9:14 LB).

A spitwad whirled through the air and splattered against Maria's neck. Joe had fired the expert shot through an inch of straw hidden in his hand.

Help! I cried silently as I walked over to Joe's desk. *God, You got me into this . . . what do I do now?*

"What's your name?" I asked this new student, pretending confidence.

"Joe," he snarled. "What's it to ya, Teach?" Coal-black eyes peered at me through matted, black hair.

"How old are you, Joe?"

"Twelve!"

"And how many years have you been in school?"

"Seven!" he snapped.

"Joe, I can't tell you how bad I feel. To think that you've been in school seven years and you don't even know how to make a good spitwad."

"Wha-a-a-t?"

"Joe, that's got to be one of the worst spitwads I've ever seen. I'll tell you what. You're going to come into my room for twenty minutes at lunch the rest of the week, and I'm going to teach you how to make *good* spitwads."

"Are you crazy, lady?"

"Be here!"

Sitting down at my desk, I thought, *What a way to start my first day at a new school.* As the students filed out at the end of class, I searched their faces. These seventh-and eighth-graders were too young to look so hardened. Their conversation wasn't the normal, warm chatter; instead, their words assaulted each other like karate chops. They were too young to be so bitter.

Peeling green paint punctuated the walls of my dismal classroom. Signs of past spitwad showers dotted the walls and blackboards—even the ceiling!

Why am I here?

Remembering my discoveries from last week's faculty meetings, I shuddered at the reasons for this school's large turnover of teachers:

The 6'2" social studies teacher, knocked to the floor by an angry student.

The English teacher, sprayed with a fire hose while she was lecturing.

The math teacher, bombarded by thirty handfuls of Twinkies the kids had smuggled into the classroom.

The entire community rattled with the kids' boasts of filling a nearby mental hospital with their teachers. The faculty had verified that two former colleagues were patients, and credited the kids with their emotional collapse.

And this is the school where God wants me?

Although I'd never wanted to be a teacher, when God directed me, I added education classes to my college major and got a teaching credential. After graduate school, I decided on the "ideal job," and earnestly prayed for it as I went job-hunting. When I was offered a teaching position that suited my design, I thanked God for the opportunity and jumped through the open door.

But, as the year progressed, I felt God nudging me. . . . *Just because a door is open doesn't mean you are to walk through it. Check with Me, Glaphré. Always make sure it is a door I have chosen for you.*

At the conclusion of my first year of teaching, when God said, *Resign,* I did. I really wanted God to be in charge, so I went looking for *His* job. *His* open door.

Each time I was offered a job . . . God said no.

August. School starts in a month. A job offer. This one I don't need to pray about. I don't need to ask God; I already know I want no part of it! Refusing to consider the offer, I assure the personnel director that the job does not fit me.

If you stray from the road to right or left you shall hear with your own ears a voice behind you saying, This is the way; follow it (Isa. 30:21 NEB).

Unable to sleep that night, I began praying, more to fill the time than for any other reason. The more I prayed, the more it seemed the job offer that day had been "God's job." I couldn't believe it! Having to teach was one thing, but this. . . ?

God, what do I know about teaching chorus and drama? I argued. *What kind of real teaching can I do in a community with a gang structure . . . student violence . . . drugs? I have no experience or desire to work with kids who pull knives on students and guns on teachers. This clearly isn't the job for me!*

But God insisted.

You know how sometimes you tell God yes, hoping that will be the end of it? That's what I did. I said yes . . . but I didn't really mean it. *Surely by morning God will forget His request,* I thought.

He didn't.

Reluctantly the next morning I phoned the personnel director of the school district and told him I'd changed my mind and would accept the job.

Since God is supposed to know everything. . .

Why *this* school?

Didn't He know *in these circumstances*

I could never do a good job?

I could never enjoy my work?

Wriggling in among my crowded thoughts came a Scripture verse:

"And the disciples said, 'Teacher. . . .'"

It echoed, rippling around the room. I'd never thought of it before. . .

God, the Father and Holy Spirit
God, the Savior and Lord
    was also God, the *Teacher*.

In that moment, teaching became something more than it had ever been before—it became an extension of God Himself. I prayed, *God, I need You to teach through me. And please, God, since You're the Creator . . . give me some creative ways of disciplining these kids. Because, believe me, I don't know what I'm doing!*

The lunch bell jarred my thoughts, and I hunted a container for Joe to use. I found one about half the size of a shoebox. With a broken red crayon, I scribbled "Spitwads" on the side of it. Soon Joe, with disbelief still on his face, was dutifully filling the box.

When Joe's twenty minutes were up, I began separating the spitwads with a knife. "Joe, these just aren't juicy enough." Pointing to others, I admonished, "I'm sorry, those aren't nearly firm enough."

After discarding the defective spitwads, I encouraged, "Now, Joe, *these* are *good* spitwads. Try to make them all like this tomorrow."

Joe walked out of the room, shaking his head.

Friday. Lunchtime. Joe's time. Joe's tongue was hanging down past his chin, but he grinned as he handed me his box, filled with perfected spitwads. When I complimented his work, he straightened his shoulders as if receiving a medal.

I would teach at this school for three years, but I would never have another spitwad thrown in my class. As a kid was tearing paper for that gooey purpose, invariably a friend in a nearby seat would caution, "Do you know what she does if. . ."

If any of you lacks wisdom, he should ask God, who gives generously to all without finding fault; and it will be given to him (Jas. 1:5 NIV).

The three gang leaders resented the kids' positive response in class. Afraid they were losing control of their declared turf, these eighth-grade chiefs conspired to strip me of the authority they claimed was theirs alone.

Danny led the last attempt. In between classes, with about thirty students gathered as their audience, the gang chieftains strutted to the front of my room. Danny held out a paper sack. "This here's my pet rattler. How d'ya like snakes, Teach?"

No real teaching—neither of my assigned subjects nor of God—was possible without the respect of the kids. But in that moment my desire to retain their growing respect clashed with my fear of snakes. Some of the pack around me were hungry for the victory of ridicule; some of them were silently pleading with me not to be intimidated; others were waiting for the outcome of this encounter to make their decision about me.

Masking my fear, I stuck my hand into the sack and asked casually, "How long have you had the rattler, Danny?"

The snake curled around my arm as I pulled out my hand. "I think your pet wants to be my bracelet."

The gang leaders looked shocked . . . and disappointed. One of them jeered, "Ah, that doesn't count! She knew it was a garter snake." Only then did I discover the snake wasn't poisonous.

Driving home that day, I realized how foolish I had been. But with the snake incident, the gang leaders conceded defeat . . . and gradually became my friends.

A by-product of those friendships was fewer discipline hassles. One day a new student burst through the door spitting out expletives. With the bold authority a gang expects of its leader, Danny silently rose from his desk, walked to this abrasive young boy, and lifted him by his arms. While holding him in midair, Danny said in a quietly menacing voice, "Don't you *ever* talk to her that way again." And, you know, he never did.

Walking down the aisle of my classroom, I spotted a water gun on Armando's desk. "Honest, Miss G., I wouldn't shoot it in here!" Such earnest pleading from this big-framed eighth-grader.

I liked being called "Miss G." The kids had given me that nickname my third week of school. It seemed to be more than the fact that "Gilliland" was long. It seemed to be an expression of friendship. At least that's the way it sounded to me. That's the way it felt.

I picked up the small yellow water gun, wondering where Armando had gotten it. The kids usually engaged in group theft, rarely individual jobs.

There was the week all the lemons disappeared from a nearby lemon orchard; the week the neighborhood drugstores were wiped out of their label-making devices; the week the grocery stores were relieved of their frozen dinners.

This week . . . water guns! Armed for combat, the students were creating havoc at the school.

"Armando, I believe you wouldn't shoot it in here," I said, picking up his newly acquired possession. "But . . . well, you see, I think I'm the only one in the whole school without a water gun. And I feel a little left out."

Before he had a chance to respond, I thanked him for giving me the water gun and asked him to stand against the side wall until the end of class. As I continued teaching, I looked down at the yellow weapon in my hand and thought, *It's such a small one, it couldn't hold much water!*

So, while teaching the lesson, I held out my arm and started emptying the barrel on Armando. I wasn't looking at him, so I couldn't see his reaction, but I faced a roomful of stunned students with gaping mouths. They looked at Armando. They looked at each other. They looked back at me. I continued teaching as if it were a standard practice to drench students during class. Big grins slowly appeared on the faces of the kids as they relaxed with this slightly unorthodox form of discipline.

I glanced over at Armando. His face was soaked. Water was beading on his chin and slowly dripping onto a wet circle on his blue T-shirt. But I'd started it . . . so of course I *had* to finish it!

I disciplined with this leaky gun the rest of the week. If a kid began to misbehave, I'd slip the water gun from my jacket pocket, squirt him in the face and warn, "Don't do that!" The shocked student would comply immediately.

There was an unspoken testing time for the first few weeks. The kids were suspicious of me and reluctant to believe I really cared. Most adults in their world didn't.

Though I allowed quiet talking in my homeroom, I didn't understand the disapproving glances that greeted me one morning when I looked up from my desk. Heads huddled together, then turned toward me in unison. The same secret, whatever it was, seemed to be winding its way around the classroom.

I lifted my coffee cup for a sip. I didn't usually drink coffee; I had never acquired the taste for it. But I had directed a six o'clock rehearsal that morning and I thought the coffee might help me feel more alert.

"Ooh . . ." "Look . . ." "Hey . . ." The audible whispers now rumbled through the room.

"What's going on with you guys?" I asked.

Embarrassed, Charlie admitted, "We thought you were smokin'. It looked like smoke comin' from behind the books on your desk, but we just figured out it was the steam from your coffee."

I had been trying to stress with my kids the importance of being truthful. They didn't care if I smoked, but since I had told them I didn't, they thought they had caught me in a lie.

It was difficult teaching the concept of honesty to these kids. Lying was so much easier for them, and they truly believed everyone adjusted their morals to the moment. They assumed people who lived in nicer neighborhoods were just more sophisticated in their methods.

I walked around and sat on the front of my desk. "I want to tell you guys something. I can't promise never to let you down . . . always to be the person I need to be. But I've chosen the way I want to live—I'm committed to God and His Son Jesus.

"I'm still learning what it means to live for God, so if you see something in my life that doesn't match up with that commitment, I want you to tell me. But know this . . . I won't play games with you. I won't pretend with you.

"I care a lot about you. I want more for you than simply doing well in school or not getting into trouble. I want you to learn that *you are important. I* know you are, but I'm not sure *you* know it."

The bell rang, but there wasn't the usual lunging for the door.

For a moment, there was silence . . .

Silence filled with love given and received.

The testing was over.

The Lord is good and glad to teach the proper path to all who go astray; He will teach the ways that are right and best to those who humbly turn to Him . . . All the ways of the Lord are loving and faithful (Ps. 25:8–10 LB, NIV).

Chapter 2.

Whose Job Is It, Anyway?

This plan of mine is not
what you would work out (Isa. 55:8 LB).

*A*lone in my classroom, I watched the shadows of dusk playing charades on the walls.

I looked at the same peeling green paint . . . the desks mutilated by the carvings of bored students. Even in the dim light, I wondered how this room had ever seemed dismal and strange to me. I loved it here! The faculty was fun and supportive; I enjoyed the subjects I taught; and the kids . . . well, the kids were special.

How I longed to gather these kids up out of homes where they were ignored . . . or verbally demolished . . . or abused. I wanted them to be somewhere else . . . with loving families. Even with me. They were too needy, too lonely, and, no matter how tough they acted, too fragile to be stuck here. What kind of chance could they have in this environment? But I couldn't do anything about their circumstances. One person couldn't make any real difference.

I shook my head to clear it of the haunting thoughts. I was here for important business—an unresolved argument with God.

My first semester was coming to a close and it was time for our musical. I couldn't believe what God wanted me to do now. He just *couldn't* mean it!

But He did.

When my struggle ended, I still wasn't eager to carry out God's instructions. I figured there had been Stephen, who was stoned to death . . . Joan of Arc, who was burned at the stake. Now . . . me. My fate—in the hands of my own miniature mob.

"Why are you in here in the dark, Miss G.?" Robert asked, flipping on the lights. Nervous about my new assignment from God, I hadn't noticed the darkening room.

Students, with the anxious excitement of their first production, were now pouring through the door.

An hour later, I stood before 240 kids—kids I'd grown to love, kids who loved me. But I was frightened. Not of the students, nor of our first performance only thirty minutes away. No, I was afraid of what I felt God wanted me to do.

"Kids, there's . . . uh . . . something I do a lot in my life . . . I'd . . . uh . . . I'd like to pray with you." *(Oh, God, are You sure I have to do this?)*

There was the expected reaction of elbowing and snickers and looks that dared me to really do it. But I prayed. A simple, personal prayer. And the room was filled with the quietness of God's presence.

Whispers floated around the room. "Hey, I liked that." "I feel different." "Does she always talk to God like that?"

The next morning I found a note in my box from the principal. Notes asking faculty members to drop by the principal's office were a common occurrence, so I assumed this meeting would be the usual request for extra yard duty.

When I went into his office, the principal continued studying some papers on his desk as he talked. "I understand you prayed with the kids last night."

"Yes, sir."

"You're not ever to do that again," he instructed with his eyes still fixed on his work.

Nervously I answered, "Fine, sir. How do I go about resigning?"

It was not a defiant answer. Nor a courageous one. Merely a timid and scared one. I hoped I was doing the right thing.

Finally he looked up at me. "Why resign?"

"Well, sir, I feel strongly that I am to pray with the kids before productions. But I wouldn't do it against your wishes, so I guess I'll have to resign."

He tilted his chair back and looked at his twirling thumbs. He didn't want me to quit. Not because I was such a terrific teacher, but because I got along well with the kids.

Leaning forward, he pointed a pencil at me. "I'll make a deal with you," he said with a mischievous grin. "You can keep praying—not in regular classes, but before productions—until I get my first complaint. How's that?"

"That's very fair. It's a deal. Thank you."

He chuckled as I walked out of his office, for this was a community of complaining people. And since the switchboard was to be turned on in ten minutes, he thought my "praying career" had a life expectancy of about twelve minutes.

The switchboard was turned on. The day passed. The year passed. Then next year, a new principal. Nothing further was said about my praying with students.

"Miss G., you forgot to pray with us!" "Hey, we didn't do good 'cause you didn't pray!" "How come you forgot?"

At the end of my first year at this junior high, my kids were performing a musical at the neighborhood elementary schools. Since we'd be at several schools that day, I decided not to be pushy about praying with the kids, and only prayed before the first assembly. They were now informing me that the second assembly wasn't as good as the first because we hadn't prayed together.

As I listened to their admonitions, I smiled inside. *Okay, God, so You knew what You were doing.*

At the end of the last performance of our version of *You're a Good Man, Charlie Brown*, the cast called me to the front. They knew they had done well and their beaming faces lit up the stage.

Opening the small box they presented to me, I unwrapped a tiny, glass-blown Snoopy.

"Look what he's doin', Miss G.," the kids cheered.

"Yeah, look!"

Snoopy was on his knees, with his head down and his front paws clasped. Snoopy was praying.

I will instruct you (says the Lord) and guide you along the best pathway for your life; I will advise you and watch your progress (Ps. 32:8 LB).

Our new principal was an ex-Marine with an old-fashioned burr haircut. He was to make a dramatic difference in our school by being a consistent and fair disciplinarian with the students, and by being supportive of the faculty. He looked up as I entered his office.

"Mr. Moore, I don't understand about this hour of counseling that's listed on my schedule for third period. I don't know anything about counseling."

"Please call me Wally," he said, leaning forward and smiling easily. "We needed someone to work with our most troublesome girls. I asked around and you were recommended for the job, so I got permission from the district for you to counsel. It only involves working with seven or eight girls."

I walked out of Wally's office wondering, *Why? After one year, I'm finally comfortable with the kids, the school, the job. So, why this?*

Those "few girls" Wally assigned me turned into a large number of boys and girls. Unbathed bodies in unwashed clothes. Many of them were emotionally, physically, or sexually abused at home. Some had hurt for so long that a numbing of their personalities seemed to be the only protection.

Eventually, all a kid needed to tell a teacher was, "I need to see Miss G.," and he was automatically excused to my room. Once I counted seventy-six students in a room set up for thirty-six.

The counseling became an opportunity to say to these kids,

"When it seems like no one cares (and for many of them, no one did), remember I care. But my caring can only make a small difference. There's a God Who cares. And *He can make all the difference.*"

Thou dost guide me with thy counsel (Ps. 73:24 RSV).

In the office was a ream of green referral slips from teachers complaining about Felix's incessant talking in class. I sent for him and introduced him to my students.

"Class, Felix is going to give a three-minute speech on the topic of his choice. You can do anything you like while he talks, except *listen!* If I catch you listening to Felix, you're in trouble with me."

Felix began expounding on the virtues of baseball. His words collided with the sound of kids talking, blowing bubbles, laughing, walking around. A quartet, huddled in one corner, was chanting an Indian war song. Some kids were even napping. His voice got louder and higher as his frustration grew.

"Miss G.!" Felix screamed over the thunderous clamor in the room, "I can't stand it. No one's listening!"

"You have one more minute to go, Felix," I insisted.

He tried, but couldn't finish. While the class resumed their assignment, Felix and I talked about how his teachers felt when he didn't listen to them.

The faculty reported a definite, although not totally consistent, improvement.

Exploding in class was a common reaction for Debbie. Anything at all seemed to set off this pretty, slim eighth-grader. Her volatile outbursts were so disruptive that as we tried to work with the cause, it was imperative that something control its results.

Deb brought me her favorite record which I kept set up on a small record player in my closet. When Deb felt the rage building within her, she'd ask to be excused to my room. She would plug in the record player, take it through my door, and once outside, perform a frenzied dance. When Deb had calmed down and was in control again, she'd put the record player back into the closet, wave good-by to me, and return to her class. The first week Deb appeared several times a day. After a month, she only had to dance away her anger once every few weeks.

Be a good teacher, tolerant, and gentle when discipline is needed (2 Tim. 2:25 NEB).

The boy waiting for me was so thin he looked emaciated. His face was expressionless. I took the green slip from his hand.

STUDENT: Richard Martinez
PROBLEM: He upset my class by sticking pencils in his ears and hair, taping a piece of paper to his neck, and sticking out his arms. He said he was a tree! With a cat stuck in its branches, no less! He wouldn't stop! I can't take any more of him!

I had to struggle not to laugh over the event which triggered this angrily written note. After we dealt with the disobedience, I urged Richard to transfer to my drama class. He became my most creative "star."

Victor was hesistant to explain why he slept through most of his classes, but eventually I learned. Night after night, he lay in bed listening to the noise from the next room where his mother conducted her business of prostitution. Victor would get so upset that he couldn't sleep.

As a supplement to our times together, I rearranged Victor's schedule. He reported first thing each morning to the nurse's office for his new elective: two hours of sleep! He improved rapidly in his other classes.

Ricky's teachers were fed up with his foul language. They complained that every time he opened his mouth, "gutter" talk spewed out.

"Ricky, I know you're not trash. But evidently *you* think you are. I want you to report here sixth period each day and sit in this trash can. Not *on* it, *in* it. When you decide you want to start acting like the person you really are, instead of like something that belongs in this can, let me know."

It started out as a lark for Ricky. He would partially disappear into the trash can, with his legs dangling out at the knees, and his arms dragging on the floor. But as the novelty wore off, he seemed to be doing some thinking.

"Miss G., you said that . . . uh . . . I mean, do you really think that . . . uh . . . well, that I shouldn't talk like I do because . . . uh, you think I'm an okay guy?"

It was a beginning.

Knowing God results in every kind of understanding (Prov. 9:10 LB).

Why is it that, even when trying to follow God's plan, we so often don't want to let go of the blueprint *we* designed?

Is it because we crafted it so carefully that we hate to waste the work?

Is it habit . . . something we don't even realize we're doing?

Is it that letting go means relinquishing control . . . and we aren't sure we want to give that up?

Or . . . is it that somewhere inside there's a belief that *our* plan is our best chance for fulfillment. Nothing God would come up with could possibly compare. So, stubbornly, we hang on.

I had been trying to hang onto my old ideas of what a teaching job should be for me—attempting to mold these circumstances into my old design.

I didn't want to let go.
  Not of my plans
    nor of my belief that *I* knew what I needed.

I still thought it was circumstances that made the difference. And these circumstances didn't fit *me*.

As if I'd never heard it before, God reminded me . . . this was *His* plan, not mine. It would work only if I did it *His way*.

Then God assured me, I could do nothing about the circumstances of my kids.

But *He* . . . God . . .
God, the Teacher
God, the Counselor
   . . . would make up the difference.
And He'd do part of it through me, if I'd let Him.

His name shall be called . . . Counselor (Isa. 9:6 KJV).

Chapter 3.

I Almost Missed It!

Fill the valleys; level the hills;
straighten out the crooked paths
and smooth off the rough spots in the road (Isa. 40:4 LB).

---

*E*ach newly revealed step of God's plan required new reliance on Him. I studied Scriptures on wisdom and prayed for that promised gift to be manifested in my work, in me—beyond my own understanding, beyond my own experience, beyond my education. I needed God to counsel through me.

Jesus the Teacher, Jesus the Counselor didn't always do what was expected of Him. But He always did what was needed.

God, what do these kids need?

As I tried to follow Jesus' pattern, I saw God open hearts, create ties of respect and caring, until . . .

some believed in themselves.
some discovered God.

What they needed . . . was to learn to have fun without being malicious. Their pranks were cruel; their jokes, destructive.

I walked to the place where the metal music stand I used as a podium was supposed to be. I pretended not to notice its absence as I placed my teaching notes on the stand. The papers fluttered to the floor.

"Okay! Okay! what have you done with it *this* time?"

On Monday the music stand had been hidden in the back of

the room. The next day, in the closet. The next, outside. Yesterday it had been on the roof.

The class worked at controlling their impish grins. With the command of a military officer, Marcedo rose from his desk and marched toward me. He placed a three-quarter-inch bolt in my hand.

"Oh no . . . don't tell me!" I laughed.

One by one, the students brought the disassembled pieces and placed them in a pile on my desk.

I clapped, applauding their creativity. Still laughing, the entire class stood and took a bow.

"Now, you know I'm not exactly a mechanical wizard. So who's going to put this back together for me?"

Three boys quickly reassembled it.

This mutual participation in a prank took only three to four minutes of each day. I struggled with taking school time for such activities. But I was beginning to understand why God had me teaching electives, for they allowed greater freedom than the required curriculum of academic subjects. It seemed more important that these kids learn they could have fun without hurting people and property than to learn an extra song.

So I played jokes on them and allowed them to play jokes on me. Together we planned grand schemes to pull on a few consenting teachers.

One opportunity came the day our principal and vice-principal were away from school attending a meeting. They were uneasy that both of them would be gone at the same time, and bombarded us with instructions. The teachers' message slots in the office sprouted bulletins from our administrators:

"George will be in charge on Friday."

"Take all problems to George on Friday."

"Although George will be teaching his math class, you are to take *all* problems of *any* kind to George in his room on Friday."

We liked George . . . but, oh, those bulletins! It just didn't seem right to let such an opportunity go by uncelebrated.

Fellow teachers—Rich, Carol, Tisha, Jim—and I began fifth period by handing out the dreaded "green slips" to our students. With delighted giggles, each student filled out his own office referral. They quietly formed a single line and, one by one, all 163 of them filed through George's class and handed him the slips.

At first George greeted the kids with bewilderment. Then, piecing the scenario together, George swallowed his smile, put on his most "official" pose, and acted as if he'd actually summoned this throng of "wrongdoers." The kids relished the prank for days.

No matter how carefully teachers guarded their supply, pencils disappeared quickly. So whenever I got a pencil, I stuck it in my hair where no one would steal it. The only problem was, I'd often forget it was there.

One day I turned from the blackboard to face my class. There sat forty-one somber, composed kids with hands folded neatly on their desks. Sticking out of each head . . . as if it had grown there . . . was a pencil. Never before had this school had so many writing utensils on its premises at one time. The pencil-decorated students were so proud of their elaborate gag. I loved the moment. I loved more that they were learning to have creative, positive fun.

You sent your good Spirit to instruct them (Neh. 9:20 LB).

What they needed . . . was to be touched.

So . . . a gentle yank of the hair. A pat on the shoulder. Straightening a collar. And the kids responded.

I didn't know this slightly built boy with torn, dirty clothes who had just appeared at my side. He seemed so shy that I had the feeling he'd run away if I spoke. But it wasn't my imagination that he was walking down the sidewalk to my classroom. I looked at him . . . smiled . . . made a fist, and lightly punched him in the stomach. Embarrassed, he looked down and walked away.

This ritual continued every day for an entire semester. His walking off was soon preceded by a nod. Then a smile. And finally, conversation. But our good-by remained the friendly stomach punch.

Little children, let us stop just saying *we love people; let us* really *love them, and* show *it by our* actions *(1 John 3:18 LB).*

What they needed . . . was success in some positive activities. Most of their successes were in negative activities—drugs, theft, prostitution, fighting . . .

I taught chorus and drama. Our performances involved not only my own classes, but eventually a majority of the entire student body. Two hundred and forty kids participated in the first production. Three hundred and fifty in the second. And over four hundred in all the rest of our grandiose productions.

Even if a student were on stage for only one minute, he still got full stage make-up and was treated like a star. The faculty good-naturedly allowed rehearsals to disrupt their classes and helped with scenery and costumes. My church friends accompanied our productions on the piano and other instruments; my family praised and fed the kids; my sister and a few other members of my teen choir at church stood behind the chorus and sang the parts my kids never mastered. The community turned out for the performances in such numbers that we staged each production several times.

Kids who had no one to listen to their incessant talking—kids who had never felt a part of home or school or peer group—kids who were never hugged—never told they were special—these kids began to feel important.

During a student-directed play rehearsal, five leather-jacketed high-schoolers on motorcycles burst through the large double doors of the multipurpose room.

"What d'ya think you're doin'?" growled a boy wearing heavy chains on his wrists and neck. He was obviously proud that he could intimidate these new seventh-graders.

In the darkness they didn't see me walking up from the back of the room.

"We're rehearsing," answered a frightened Lua.

"Oh, yeah?" The boy's menacing tone sounded like a threat. "Who's your Teach?" he demanded.

"Miss G.," someone replied in a shaky voice.

"Oh, yeah? I'm one of her kids. In fact," he bragged, straightening the dirty scarf he used as a headband, "I bet I was her biggest star!"

"Well, I was in one deal," said another member of the entourage. "That makes me her kid, too!"

"I was a wise man. I'd like to see you two goons top that!" chided the leader.

"Hi, guys."

"Oh . . . oh, hi, Miss G. We didn't know you were here."

We chatted a bit, and made arrangements for a "check in"—appointments when my former students told me what was happening in their lives. They wished the cast luck and rode off on their bikes.

He will bring blind Israel along a path they have not seen before. He will make the darkness bright before them and smooth and straighten out the road ahead. He will not forsake them (Isa. 42:16 LB).

What they needed . . . was to be trusted.

"Miss G., what'll I do?" panicked Christina. "The leg on the side table just broked!"

"The production begins in three minutes and I have to stay here and direct the choir. As stage manager, that's your responsibility. You'll think of something," I answered reassuringly.

At the appropriate time there was the table, giving seemingly sturdy support to the two boys standing on it.

The next day when I opened the closet in my room, I discovered my broom no longer had a handle. Christina had certainly been "creative" in fulfilling her responsibility as stage manager.

The days of disbelief were gone. The kids knew I expected them to fulfill their responsibilities . . . that I wanted to hear their opinions . . . that I trusted them to get the change they needed out of my purse.

He will encourage the fainthearted (Isa. 42:3a LB).

What they needed . . . was to learn to be thoughtful of others.

Sixty to eighty kids stood in a loosely formed group and yelled taunts and jeers at Cal. A frequent occurrence.

Cal, who was in Special Education, was extremely slow in his speech and responses. But he had appointed himself the "Campus Crier" to anyone who abused the lawn by standing on it. The other kids were merciless to him.

When Cal was transferred to chorus, he wasn't a bit shy about his off-key singing, and bellowed with great gusto. He seemed not to notice the unkind rolling of eyes and whispered ridicule.

I sent Cal on an errand while I talked to my class.

"I don't understand you. Who of you thinks he's so neat, so cool he can make fun of anyone else? I know me pretty well. And I know there's not a person on the face of the earth I have the right to make fun of.

"What do you think? That Cal doesn't know you're laughing at him? That he doesn't hurt the way you hurt? I just don't get it. You're better people than this."

When Cal returned, he had a roomful of mother hens.

"Cal, you have to stay here all day. I've told you that several times!" His Special Education teacher was growing weary of Cal's attempts to leave.

"But I'm late for choir. I'll come back later," Cal said.

Once again the teacher explained that the special testing would last all day. He wouldn't be going to any of his classes.

"You don't understand," Cal pleaded. "I *have* to go to chorus. They *like* me in there."

He will be gentle . . . He will not break the bruised reed, nor quench the dimly burning flame (Isa. 42:2 LB).

The classroom got muggy as summer approached. In the last days of the countdown before school was out, my chorus asked me to leave the room for a few minutes. As I was leaving, I checked on Gary. He had a problem with claustrophobia so, a couple of times a day, he'd come to my room. My seating chart specified a place for him out the side door by the large shade tree. The only rule was that he had to be able to touch the tree at all times. When he saw me, he wiggled his toe against the bark of the tree trunk and waved.

When the class called me back, I returned to a room filled with carefully made decorations of paper flowers and streamers; a homemade four-foot card of appreciation; eager faces of kids who were obviously pleased with what they'd done.

And . . . a gift.

"We didn't kipe it, Miss G.! Honest!"

I thought back to my first Christmas at this school. Generous students had piled a mound of presents on my desk. Then Alan had walked in and presented me with a lovely transistor record player. (Alan, a small boy with sparkling eyes, was the fence for a whole network of elementary kids who stole bicycles.)

"Alan, I can't accept this," I told him.

"How come, Miss G.?"

"Because you stole it."

"Who told ya?" he asked angrily.

"No one had to tell me."

"Miss G., you *have* to keep it! It's the hardest thing I ever kiped! Besides nobody'd know."

"Alan, *I* would know. I appreciate the thought, but every time I'd listen to it, it would bother me. I'll keep the stereo on one condition: You tell me where you got it, and I'll go pay for it."

"I don't want ya to do that. I'll get it back somehow," Alan conceded as he left with the stereo.

Throughout the remainder of the afternoon, kids had come in, saying, "Hear if we kiped your present, ya don't want it."

At the end of the day the mound of presents on my desk had dwindled to one gift.

So, the chorus was assuring me *this* gift wasn't stolen.

Inside the box was a lovely small gold cross and a note that read,

We know you're friends with God so we thought you'd like this.

The teachers later told me the kids had shared lunches for two months to save the money for my cross.

I almost missed all of that! The privilege of loving dirty-faced, unruly kids until I didn't notice those things as much as their hurts and hearts.

I almost missed it.

During my three years at that school, I prayed with all my production casts and crews before our performances—over one thousand different kids. Since many students were in numerous productions, I prayed with most of them several times. There was never one complaint.

I almost missed it.

I almost missed the opportunity for personal growth—all because I looked at *my* plans . . . and initially said no to a job I didn't think suited me.

Looking back on those three years, I have to wonder how much I crippled God's purpose for that time because I kept resisting His direction. Kept hanging onto my own perception of what was right for me.

But . . . whatever it *wasn't* . . . one thing it *was* . . . it was
   the beginning of a crucial lesson:
      It's not a plan *we* create that determines
      our fulfillment.
         It's what we let *God* do in the plan of His
         choosing.

Turn me away from wanting any other plan than Yours (Ps. 119:37 LB).

Tell me what to do, O Lord,
and make it plain . . .
Give me an understanding mind.

Get to work.
Don't be frightened by the size of the task,
for the Lord my God is with you. . . .
He will see to it that everything is finished correctly.

And this is my prayer,
that your love may grow
ever richer and richer
in knowledge and insight of every kind,
and may thus bring you the gift of true discrimination. . . .
Let the work of Christ dwell in you richly
in all wisdom.

The Lord God has given me His words of wisdom
so that I may know what I should say
to these weary ones. . . .
I will bless the Lord who counsels me;
He gives me wisdom in the night.
He tells me what to do.

(Ps. 27:11; 3:9 LB; 1 Chron. 28:20 LB;
Phil. 1:9, 10 NEB; Col. 3:16 KJV;
Isa. 50:4; Ps. 16:7 LB).

Part 2.

God Makes the Difference In Our Security

———————————————

WE LOOK AT OURSELVES—

ASSESS OUR STRENGTHS,
CRINGE AT OUR WEAKNESSES,
CONSTRUCT A BOX
AND CRAWL INSIDE.

WE TELL GOD TO MAKE A DIFFERENCE . . .

AS LONG AS WE GET TO STAY
INSIDE THE BOX.

Chapter 4.

A Place to Hide

I am with you;
that is all you need (2 Cor. 12:9 LB).

God, either You have the wrong person, or You've pulled the wrong folder out of Your file. No way could this be right for me!

I had resigned my teaching job because of illness. Now, after several months of recuperation, I felt God guiding me to be free of a job for a while (whatever that meant!) and go wherever He said, for whatever purpose He directed.

Immediately I knew God was confused, so I proceeded to help Him straighten out His mistake: *God, are You forgetting which of Your children I am? I'm the one who has no desire to travel! Remember? I want to stay in one place.*

Just in case He wasn't convinced, I had more: *My car doesn't work most of the time . . . I get lost a lot, and I can't read maps . . . I'm not outgoing enough to be with strangers all the time. And, besides, what am I supposed to do for money?*

I could see myself stranded in the desert—my car out of gas, no money—and God having to fly in a bird with a can of gas in its beak!

God's voice has never been relayed to me over the radio. I've never received a telegram signed, "The Almighty." I've never seen handwriting on the wall. Well . . . there was that one time . . . but being the quick thinker that I am, I surmised that God wouldn't use a black eyebrow pencil to inscribe His message on my wall.

Besides, my unit mates were trying too hard to be composed as I entered my dorm room and read the message they had scribbled on my wall in huge letters:

> Glaphré:
> You must preach!
>   The Lord

God's main way of communicating with me has always been through His Word—with His Holy Spirit interpreting Scripture, giving me direction, inspiration, correction, and comfort. So, I looked in my Bible, hoping to find a way out of this. Hoping it wasn't really God.

Show me the path where I should go, O Lord; point out the right road for me to walk. . . . How I need a map—and your commands are my chart and guide. . . . Guide me clearly along the way you want me to travel so that I will understand you and walk acceptably before you (Ps. 25:4, 119:19; Ex. 33:13 LB).

And the Lord replied, I myself will go with you . . . Do not worry about what to say. . . . At that time you will be given what to say (Ex. 33:14 LB; Matt. 10:19 NIV).

God waited until I'd finished pleading my case. . . . Then He began the lesson of the box.

My children get so mixed up. You think what you become depends on what you see in yourselves: your abilities . . . or lack of them; your opportunities . . . or lack of them; your successes or failures.

Those things don't determine what happens in you and through you. It's what you allow Me to be in you that makes the difference.

But, you don't believe it. You believe more in what you aren't than in what I AM.

God reminded me of the illiterate, tongue-tied cowboy my grandmother had told me about. He attended his first church service in his only clothing—ragged overalls, boots with no socks, and a soiled, gray cowboy hat. At the end of the service He responded to the invitation and gave his heart to Jesus.

Now, no one would expect God to do much with this grubby cowboy. Oh, maybe he could witness to the cattle. Maybe he could even be a little better cowboy. But . . . after all, he couldn't read or write, and his speech was extremely difficult to understand.

Yet, at the turn of the century, throngs of people traveled hundreds of miles in wagons to hear the man they called "Uncle Buddy" Robinson preach. Thousands of people found Christ through the ministry of this humble man.

This cowboy preacher must have known what God was trying to teach me. He must have believed that what he became wasn't determined by his limitations, but by what he allowed God to be in him.

God says: *"I AM THAT I AM" (Ex. 3:14 KJV).*

But we often reject that truth, and reply:

No, God, *I am.*
   I am shy.
   I am untalented.
   I am alone.

God declares, *"I AM THAT I AM."*

We interrupt Him,

No, God,
   I am . . .

And we begin constructing a box. A box with a protective nook for each of our weaknesses . . . each of our fears . . . each of our strengths . . . each of our self-made plans. A comfortable hiding place.

"I AM THAT I AM."

No God,
    You don't understand. *I am*.
        I am not very smart.
        I am a failure.
        or
        I am really good at *these* things.
        I am going to accomplish all *my* goals.

God keeps trying to get our attention off ourselves . . . but we've found our niche, and we're *so sure* it's right. After all, each of us has designed our box to fit perfectly. We wear it into each moment, each new opportunity, each situation—our box is our security.

When a heart truly desires to surrender totally to God, it cries out:

Here I am, God.
Take me.
Use me.
I'm all Yours!

But as God begins to do just that, some of us add, "Oh, by the way, God . . . there are a few things You need to realize about me:

I've never done anything like *this* before.
I could never be used in *this* way.
I know exactly what I want to do with my life!
I'm really busy.

Then we slap the lid on our box with "That's just the way *I am,* God. I can't help it! But, take me. I'm all Yours."

And God does just that. He takes us . . . box and all.

I could sense how much I was grieving God, as I felt Him saying,

Why don't you understand?
You don't need the box.
   YOU HAVE ME!

God had asked me to accept an assignment that was contrary to everything I wanted to do, an assignment which required strengths I did not possess. Resisting the Holy Spirit's leading demonstrated that a part of my security came from hiding within limits I had set around my life. I didn't like admitting I was afraid to trust God enough to cross those limits.

My friend Gloria understands this truth. It's still difficult for Gloria to believe God uses her in the ministry of music. Sometimes she wants to say, "God, use me somewhere else. I'm not comfortable with this." But her commitment to God gives Him freedom to direct her life in whatever way He chooses. She relies on God to equip her to sing to His glory. To write music that comforts and encourages. To share His message.

Gloria believes more in what God can do in her and through her, than in what she considers her inadequacies.

I'm grateful she considers total dependency on God necessary for her ministry. For without it, today we wouldn't enjoy the music of Bill and Gloria Gaither.

And God said . . . 'I AM THAT I AM.'

I felt God saying, *Glaphré, how I long for you to understand.*
   You don't need that box.
   What you become does not have to depend upon you.

> *Not on what you can or can't do.*
>   *Not on what you think you will*
>   *or will never be.*
>   *I will make the difference, if you'll let Me.*

There was the crux of it! I wasn't looking at *God* at all. I was looking at *me*.

I am the Lord your God, who teaches you what is best for you, who directs you in the way you should go (Isa. 48:17 NIV).

Chapter 5.

Climbing Out of My Box

Lord, don't let me make
a mess of things (Ps. 119:31 LB).

---

*A*ttempting to see beyond my limitations, I accepted God's assignment:

I was to travel.
    To go where God directed.
        When He directed.
            For whatever purpose He revealed.

Further, I was never to tell anyone about any financial need, not even my parents. No credit cards. No checkbook. I was to tell God alone, and He would supply the need.

I'd been asking God to teach me what it meant to depend on Him. But this answer seemed a bit extreme.

God brought Matthew to my mind. That disciple could have said, "Jesus, I want to follow You, but I have an awful reputation. Even though You've forgiven and changed me, my past will hinder Your ministry. I'd better not travel with You. Thanks for asking me, though."

Follow Me, he told him, and Matthew got up and followed Him (Matt. 9:9 NIV).

Jesus could have said, "I'm Your Son, You can't ask this of me. I won't do it!" And we wouldn't have God's gift of salvation or Jesus' life of obedience as our example.

Your attitude should be the kind that was shown us by Jesus Christ, who, though He was God, did not demand and cling to His rights as God. . . . Although He was a Son, He learned obedience from what He suffered and, once made perfect, He became the source of eternal salvation for all who obey Him (Phil. 2:5 LB; Heb. 5:8, 9 NIV).

Nervously, I opened my box.

Because I'd struggled for weeks with this unconventional assignment, I expected my family to have the same problem with it.

"I don't understand it and I don't know how long I'll be traveling," I explained. In an attempt at reassurance—as much for myself as for them—I read them all the Scriptures God had used to direct me. I had formed this mental image of my family, distraught over such a strange turn in my life. I should have known God isn't haphazard in His planning. He had prepared my family, too. Each of them had felt God would be leading me into something "different." It was different, all right!

Before I left on this new venture, I took my teaching contract out of my dresser drawer. When I had tried to resign, my school district had insisted I take a leave of absence instead. I held the contract in my hand . . . I wanted to hang onto it . . . just in case. . . .

I had always considered my money God's. When we were small children, Dad had handed us tithing envelopes along with our weekly allowance. One of our ten pennies was to be our tithe—God's Word said we were to give it back to Him. Since all of our money really belonged to God, we could decide if we wanted to give more. We felt important having tithing envelopes just like our parents did. Opening the Gilliland kids' envelopes of pennies each week was probably a nuisance for the church treasurer. But because of it, tithing has never been a problem for us as adults.

Even so, I'd never had to *depend* on God for my finances. I had my salary. And Dad was always there if I needed him.

Tell Me.
Listen to Me.
Trust Me.
I AM *your provision.*

With shaky confidence in God's promise, I tore up the contract. My security needed to come from trust in God alone, not in a contingency plan in case God didn't come through. For the same reason, I left Dad's credit cards on his nightstand. I didn't leave a note. He'd know why I couldn't accept his offer.

And if God provides clothing for the flowers that are here today and gone tomorrow, don't you suppose that He will provide clothing for you, you doubters? (Luke 12:28 LB).

New Jersey. My blue Volkswagen crept up the hill. At least it was making some progress, even if I did have the urge to pedal. I didn't know why I was here. I wasn't even sure it was where God wanted me, but I decided I'd rather go and be wrong, than *not go* and be wrong!

With my usual lack of expertise, I parallel-parked my car on the main street of a small town. After several attempts, the car was still crooked, but at least it was fairly close to the curb. I stood on the sidewalk wondering why I was here. I'd never been to New Jersey before. I didn't know anyone in the whole state.

"Hey lady! Have a joint?" Two brown eyes peered through long, greasy hair. The boy repeated his question. "I said, 'D'ya have a joint?' "

This lanky teenager acted like a tired, old man. "I don't have any marijuana," I answered. "But I have something else I'd like to share with you."

Sitting on the curb, I asked God to interpret Burt's conversation. To help me know what was real . . . what was said for effect. To say through me what this confused boy needed to hear. I was grateful God could untangle thoughts and feelings.

An hour later, I walked with Burt to a phone booth.

"Don't cry, Mom." As Burt consoled his mother, his own tears fell freely. "I'm okay, really I am. . . . Yeah, I'm coming home now."

Burt waved as he boarded the bus. In five hours he would be reunited with his Christian family who hadn't know his whereabouts for the past three months.

Two hours after I had parked my car in that small, bleak New Jersey town, I was on the road again. It had been God's voice after all. The mission was completed.

For the Lord God says: I will search and find My sheep . . . I will seek My lost ones, those who strayed away, and bring them safely home again . . . (Ezek. 34:11, 16 LB).

I wanted God's guidance to arrive effortlessly. Neatly and clearly packaged. And if the package wasn't delivered *immediately,* I wasn't secure enough in God to *wait* for Him. So, I'd figure out what to do myself.

If you needed your dad's advice, would you call him, state the problem, ask for advice, then hang up? God asked me. *If you wouldn't do that to your dad, why do it to Me?*

Good question. I was ashamed of the answer. I knew Dad would come through. I guess I wasn't always sure God would. So I studied Scriptures which declared God's desire to guide His children.

But when He, the Spirit of truth comes, He will guide you into all truth . . . You guide me with your counsel (John 16:13; Ps. 73:24 NIV).

God help me be secure in Your guidance. With that prayer I made a commitment:

Not to race for God's guidance,
   but to seek it
      until I found it.
         I would not move ahead without it.

It was a lot slower. A lot more trouble. But what a difference that security made.

Tennessee. The interstate—or rather the shoulder of the interstate. My car had broken down again. (I kept asking God to heal it, but He never did!) It was a nice day, and I was sitting on the ground outside my car, looking at the wildflowers growing along the side of the road.

A large truck pulled over and two men got out. I smiled, thinking of the multitude of truckdrivers and service station attendants I had met across the country—all because I had no sense of direction and an ailing car. Or was it really part of God's mission?

"Trouble?" asked the man with a red cap and tattoed arms.

"I think my car needs a doctor. How's your medical degree?"

The men laughed. In the fifteen minutes they worked on my car, they talked freely of their dissatisfaction with life. I shared with them what I knew to be the answer.

The two men bent under the tilted hood of my car, doing whatever you do to uncooperative engines, while I remained seated on the ground. As I talked, the men glanced up from the engine more and more often, until they stopped working and leaned against the car's blue frame. They were listening . . . listening to a stranger tell them of a God who could make a difference in their lives.

"You got anything on this stuff?" This truckdriver looked older. And bigger. And lonelier.

"I've got a road map," I answered as I retrieved two Bibles from the back of my car. One clear directive from God was to carry Bibles with me and give them to whomever He directed.

"Even though we got your car started," one of the truckers hollered out his window, "you need to go straight to a station and get it fixed."

"Thanks for your help. I really appreciate it."

"No. Thank *you!*" said the older man, waving the Bible.

My word . . . will achieve the purpose for which I sent it (Isa. 55:11 NIV).

Ohio. Sunday morning. I stopped at a small community church to worship. This white-steepled building housed thirty or forty people—men in overalls, women in hats, kids peering over the backs of pews. All singing with loud joy. After the hymn, the pastor requested that the congregation pray for a Mrs. Miller, who was in the hospital.

Back on the highway, I still felt the warmth of the little congregation with big music in their hearts. I prayed again for Mrs. Miller.

I'm going to touch her, I felt God saying. *I want you to go pray with her.*

God . . . get real! I don't even know who she is. Or where she is.

I'm going to heal her. You're to pray with her.

I drove over to the side of the road, stopped the car and wrestled with God. Reluctantly I conceded . . . yet I felt I was to continue driving *away* from the city where the church was located.

An hour's drive down the highway, I exited the ramp—not at all convinced I was following God's direction.

I pulled into the first service station. "Is there a hospital near here?" I asked the attendant.

There was . . . six blocks away.

Parked in the hospital parking lot, I got out my reliable, protective box and crawled inside. *God what if this isn't You? What if I mess You up? What if I embarrass You? . . . I don't even know this woman's first name!*

Don't trust in your own experience. Trust in Me.

Still scared, I opened the car door and got out. Walking into the hospital, I prayed, *God, if this isn't Your idea . . . I mean if it's some crazy scheme* I've *dreamed up . . . please . . .* please *stop it at the front desk.*

The hospital receptionist hung up the phone and checked the card file. "Mrs. Miller is in Room 233, but her husband is the only visitor allowed."

I was so *relieved!* Grateful for my reprieve, I walked out of the hospital, but paused just outside the entrance. Standing there, I looked back through the huge glass doors and thought, *I didn't know her first name or her husband's name . . . but I still ended up with a room number. I might as well check it out.*

The door of Room 233 was propped open, and a man who appeared to be in his sixties was sitting by the bed. He motioned for me to come in.

I identified myself and told him how I'd heard of his wife's condition. "If it's all right with you, I'd like to pray for her."

He eagerly accepted the offer. When we finished praying, his face reflected that he felt God's presence. Immediately after the prayer, I left.

I didn't know what was wrong with Mrs. Miller. I didn't know what God had done. I didn't know that six months later in another state, a college president whom I'd never met before would say in introducing me to his student body:

"My wife and I have some good friends who are very influential in the area of Ohio from which we come. However, they were not Christians and had adamantly refused to discuss their spiritual condition with anyone. Last year, when Mrs. Miller was lying in the hospital in critical condition, a stranger stopped by her room and prayed with her. After I heard about it, I rushed to the hospital, afraid the Millers' reaction would be negative.

"When I got there, Mrs. Miller was greatly improved, and Mr. Miller said, 'That young lady knew whom she was talking to when she prayed.'

"God touched Mrs. Miller. The severe hemorrhaging stopped and she is fine today.

"The young woman who prayed for Mrs. Miller is our speaker today."

As I drove away from the hospital, I didn't know God would allow me the privilege of finding out what He'd done for Mrs. Miller. I just knew I'd left my box in the car and trusted God.

Tell me what to do, O Lord, and make it plain (Ps. 27:11 LB).

A giant quilt of overstuffed white clouds patched the blue sky outside the window of the plane.

I felt safe. Not because the clouds looked soft. Not because the plane was working well. But because I was learning to trust in God instead of in my box.

"Please fasten your seat belts," requested the flight attendant. "We are preparing for our descent to Barbados."

This Caribbean trip, another of God's ideas, had seemed impossible to me. The cost of the airfare and motels, plus other traveling expenses, would require money I didn't have. But by now I knew better than to argue with God. I was learning.

I'd been traveling by car for eight months. My retirement money from teaching had financed the first few months, then I was out. But God wasn't.

The money was provided in small sums, dribbling in at just the right moment. Often at the very *last* moment.

A stranger would stop me on the street. "I think I'm supposed to give you this," she'd say, handing me twenty dollars.

At the cash register in a restaurant, I'd discover someone had already paid for my meal. Only once was the person still there so I could thank him.

While staying with friends, the doorbell would ring. "Do you have a guest? This is for her." My bewildered hosts gave me the white envelope containing fifty dollars.

I'd get something out of my purse and discover some extra money, never knowing who had slipped it into my purse during the day.

People's sensitivity to God's leading was amazing to me. Their obvious belief that their money was God's to spend, ministered to me even more than the money itself.

Don't trust either in money or the lack of it.
Trust in Me.

He will always give you all you need from day to day if you will make the Kingdom of God your primary concern (Luke 12:31 LB).

One week after I made my reservation for the Caribbean, I received a check for the entire airfare. My ticket was open, with no specific destination printed on it. For three weeks I would be flying to different islands as God directed.

Same game plan.

Different location.

Whoever trusts in the Lord is kept safe (Prov. 29:25 NIV).

Chapter 6.

Life on the Outside

I will freely do what the Father
requires of me so that the world will
know that I love the Father. *Come, let's be going* (John 14:31 LB).

*B*arbados lived up to all my idyllic images of a beautiful island. Clean white sand. Blue water. Tall palm trees.

On my second day in Barbados, I decided to see some of the island and learned the most economical way would be the well-organized island bus system. At the town square, I looked for a friendly face. A beautiful, statuesque woman with short-cropped hair, who was speaking English to several men, smiled at me. I asked her advice on which bus to take.

"I show you."

She walked with me several blocks to the bus stop. Then, afraid I would get lost in the unfamiliar setting, she decided to ride part of the way with me.

As the bus buzzed with the people's unrecognizable chatter, Jasmine communicated with her dark expressive eyes and a reserved poise.

The view from the bus window was a blend of contrasts: colorful Western and native dress; bicycles rolling past women carrying bundles on their heads; the pensive stares of the elderly, punctuated by the energetic glee of playful kids.

"How old you think I am?" Jasmine asked. I guessed twenty-two. She said she was forty.

"I get off here." I thanked her for her kindness. "Your name hard. Say again."

Laughing at the familiar response to my strange name, I took some paper from my purse and wrote it out for her. Adding the name and address of my motel, I handed the paper to her as I pronounced my name again.

When Jasmine got off the bus and waved good-by to me, I prayed for her.

Two days later, the jarring ring of the phone in my motel room surprised me. Who would be calling me here in Barbados?

"Hello, this Jasmine. You lady I meet on bus? I come see you today. Is okay?"

"I'd love for you to visit me. Do you know how to get to my motel?"

"Yes. I take bus. I bring daughters. Is okay?"

"Your daughters are welcome. What time will you be here?"

"Four o'clock."

Jasmine arrived in a colorful, crisp cotton dress. Her eleven- and twelve-year-old daughters kept staring at the ground, so I knelt down in front of them. I looked into round faces, lonely eyes, and slicked-back hair braided with bright red ribbons.

"They never meet American before. I want them meet you," Jasmine explained.

After consuming their requested French fries and Cokes, the girls wanted another first—television. There was a set in my room.

With the girls captured by a "Superman" rerun, Jasmine and I sat by the pool and talked.

"You tell me more about this God you say about on bus."

During our talk, Jasmine turned her head away. "You not think God love me if you know."

When she was fifteen, Jasmine had been sent to England to be the housekeeper and mistress of an elderly man. When she was eighteen, the man died and she was returned to Barbados. Since that time she had made her living as a prostitute.

"Jasmine, look at me. . . . Can you see that what you've told me makes no difference? Can you see I still want to be your friend?"

Jasmine studied my face, then nodded.

"If I were to tell you things about my dad, would you believe me? Things like . . . what color his hair is . . . what makes him laugh . . . how he treats me. . . . Would you believe me?"

"Yes," she answered quietly.

"Could you believe me if I told you he would want to be your friend, too?"

"He would?"

"Yes. Do you believe me?"

"You daughter. You know."

"That's right, I'm his daughter and I know him . . . Jasmine, when I became a Christian I became God's daughter, and I've learned to know *Him,* too.

"God is love. So what He feels for you has to be love. It doesn't matter what a person has done wrong. Jesus' gift of salvation is for *anyone* who asks.

"I'm God's daughter. I know He wants you to be His daughter, too." The months of learning to know my God and His love—without my box—added credibility to a message that was already truth.

We talked candidly of alternate lifestyles—other ways she could support her family. I asked her to think about it seriously.

"I do it."

We prayed for God to help her with her decision.

"My girls, too, please."

When we went back inside the room, the girls' eyes remained riveted on the television set as they greeted us. I gave them each a Bible and began talking to them. More and more their attention shifted from the television program, until one girl turned off the set. After an introduction to Jesus which required some translation by their mother, they allowed me to pray for them.

As I watched them walk away with their arms intertwined, I

prayed, *Oh, God, please protect them.* I smiled at the gift I was holding—a hat Jasmine had crocheted for me. This purple-and-black tam was about the right size for a toddler, but it was very special to me. I'd always keep it.

I, the Lord, will tend the fruitful vines; every day I'll water them, and day and night I'll watch to keep all enemies away (Isa. 27:3 LB).

Except for one other opportunity, Jasmine and her girls were the only islanders I was to tell about God in the entire three weeks. God had something else in mind.

Morning by morning He wakens me and opens my understanding to his will (Isa. 50:4 LB).

On my last night in Barbados—at midnight—I had the urge to take an impromptu swim. It never occurred to me it might be God's direction.

The water in the swimming pool felt cool and refreshing. I was enjoying the quiet moments of solitude.

"Look at that adventuresome person!" yelled someone, pointing at me. I turned and saw a group of four young couples approaching the pool area. "How about it? Anyone game?" The voice challenging his friends belonged to a sandy-haired man in his early twenties.

A few minutes later three of the group plunged into the water with me. They were medical students from Canada, vacationing during a term break.

Dick, the sandy-haired one, and I soon learned that we shared a love for the ocean. Since it was only a few feet away, Dick suggested we swim there.

The water looked unusually calm. Even so, it would take strength I didn't have. But God was prompting me to go into the ocean with Dick, so my strength would have to be *His* problem.

The soft tumbling surf created a relaxing background for conversation as we swam leisurely in the blue-black water.

"Can you see the shore?" Dick asked suddenly.

"I've never been able to see it. Can't see much of anything without my glasses. Why?"

"We've drifted out pretty far." There was an edge of alarm in his voice.

I prayed for strength as we began swimming for shore.

"I don't think we've made any progress at all!" Dick's confident, worldly-wise tone was gone. "I guess we just keep trying. At least we're not drifting further out," he said, trying to be reassuring.

Dick was panting from his struggle with the undertow. I was so tired I just wanted to quit and float wherever the current took me.

"You're not scared, are you?" He was panicky now—and almost angry that I wasn't. "How come you're not scared? We're fighting for our lives! How can you be so calm?"

I know it sounds crazy, but . . .

in the ocean
    at one o'clock in the morning
        off the beach of Barbados
            fighting for survival
                a medical student from Canada
                heard about a God who could bring
                peace to anyone, anywhere.

Somehow we managed to make it back to shore. Dick believes it's because we prayed together and asked God to help us. I do, too.

The next day Dick and I talked some more. He had spent the night storing up questions about a God he had never believed in. He accepted a Bible and began leafing through it.

I knew it was time to leave.

The ocean outside the plane window reminded me of Dick and the splashing witness in the middle of the night. Obedience had meant different things during this year of following wherever God led. But that was one of the most unique!

Since the Lord is directing our steps, why try to understand everything that happens along the way? (Prov. 20:24 LB).

Life outside the box had more variety than anything I could have planned for myself:

Witnessing in the ocean in Barbados.
Cleaning house for a woman in Nebraska.
Speaking at the "Quiet Time" at the University of Jamaica.
Baby-sitting for a worn-out mother in Iowa.
Listening to an elderly man's ramblings in Pennsylvania.
Praying for a man's healing in Florida.
Speaking at the conclusion of a Catholic mass in Tennessee.
Cleaning up after a bed-bound woman in California.
Shopping for a Texas couple who needed food.

When I was tempted to compare one assignment with another, to rank its importance, God cautioned against the dangers of building a box out of the world's standards for success—then gauging the importance or helpfulness of *anything* against it.

The world—even the Christian world—can applaud an action that is far from what I need it to be. Or, the world may remain silent when you fulfill something exactly as I order it. Don't trust in the response of others. Trust in Me.

I was learning . . . there isn't room inside a box for total trust in God. Maybe that's one reason the box is so popular. Comfortably tucked away within its confines, there is little demand for us to grow.

We don't see
  by shutting ourselves in,
we are also
  shutting God and His call out.

But life is worth nothing unless I use it for doing the work assigned me by the Lord Jesus—the work of telling others the Good News about God's mighty kindness and love . . . I know who it is in whom I have trusted *(Acts 20:24 LB; 2 Tim. 1:12 NEB).*

Chapter 7.

Trust—
The Secure Freedom

Your decisions are as full of wisdom
as the oceans are with water. . . .
Tell me where You want me
to go and I will go there (Ps. 36:6; 86:11 LB).

*I*t was a beautiful, sunny day in the Virgin Islands. Since I was nearing the end of my trip, I decided to take a break and go to the beach. Today I wasn't going to talk to *anyone!* I spread out the towel on the small U-shaped beach sprinkled with sunbathers, and picked up my book.

"Hi!"

I looked up to see a tall man wearing wire-rimmed glasses. Even on the beach, he looked as if he should be carrying an attaché case.

"May I sit down?"

"Sure," I answered, closing my book. Some break! I hadn't even had a chance to read one sentence.

Settling on his towel, he asked, "You having a good time?"

"Yes. It's beautiful here. How about you?"

The middle-aged man looked out at the cove full of sailboats skimming the water like colorful butterflies. "I don't know . . . I haven't found anything that really brings meaning to life. Have you?"

I fought back a smile. It was as if he had just asked, "Would you please explain the plan of salvation to me?"

The IBM executive from Texas and I talked a long time about the meaning God brings to a person's life. "I've never heard this before," he slowly admitted. "No one I know believes this."

There was that statement again. I hadn't understood why God had brought me to the Caribbean to share about Him with tourists, but each had responded with the same statement: "I don't know anyone who believes this."

Two hours later, the IBM executive became a Christian.

The next afternoon I took a walk. Leaning against the tennis court fence was Brad, my friend from the beach. He was reading the Bible I had given him. I didn't want to interrupt him, so I kept on walking.

And now I entrust you to God and to His care and to His wonderful words which are able to build your faith and give you all the inheritance of those who are set apart for Himself (Acts 20:32 LB).

"Hello, there!" Her greeting surprised me. I'd seen this elderly woman several times at the pool. Each time I had waved or spoken, her only response had been a sour expression.

This afternoon she was talking to a man in his forties. He didn't look too thrilled with life, either. She greeted me as if I were an old friend and introduced me to her son Robert. This trip was his birthday present to his mother. He interrupted their grumbling to invite me to join them for dinner, but I didn't feel like being sociable, so I declined.

In my devotional time that night, I felt God's rebuke. He had planned for me to accept Robert's dinner invitation, but I hadn't checked with God first.

The next evening I felt directed to go to a specific restaurant where I would find Robert . . . but I didn't see him anywhere. As I was walking out the door, someone tapped me on the shoulder. It was Robert!

We sat on the restaurant patio and talked. I learned that this troubled man was the photo editor of a popular American sex magazine. "People think my job sounds exciting," he said. "Sometimes it is, but usually it's boring."

I explained the difference God had made in my life. "Robert, I know God can make the same difference in your life."

"I don't know anyone in the States who believes like this," he told me, and went on to ask a lot of questions.

The next morning there was a knock on the door. It was Robert. "I'm leaving now, but I wanted to stop by and thank you for our talk. I'm thinking about it." Before he left, he accepted a Bible.

The next day on my flight back to the States, I wondered how many Brads and Roberts I'd known. How many people in my world knew nothing about God? How many times had I let negative feelings about myself keep me from sharing God? How often had I cowered inside my box and missed God's creative use of my life?

God, thank You for showing me so clearly why I have *to focus on You.*

I looked at the Bible in my hand. It was my last one.

Some friends had given me sixty Bibles for my birthday.

One hundred and fifty Bibles had been left on my parents' front porch with an unsigned note: "These are for Glaphré."

A phone call came from a man I'd never met. While buying paint in a store in Oklahoma City, he had overheard a couple discussing my year of traveling. There—in the paint store—God had spoken to him and he had ordered 250 Bibles for me.

And now . . . there was only one.

"We ask all our passengers to please fasten your seat belts. We'll be landing in Miami in fifteen minutes."

More than this one trip was ending. This was also to be the conclusion of my traveling assignment.

Driving back to my parents' home in Oklahoma, I felt like a

toddler who'd been carried from person to person . . . from place to place . . . from situation to situation. Each time God had said,

Look Who I AM, *Glaphré.*
Look what I *can do.*
You don't need that box.
I AM.

I knew now . . . I couldn't obey God unless I listened to Him. I had to "hear" what God wanted me to do.

But the box . . . the box muffled what I heard and restricted my obedience. It kept my eyes on *me* instead of on God. It fastened part of my security on circumstances, on self-limitations and personal desires—shabby substitutes for God's offer of safety in Him.

I didn't need to hide in my box because of what I *wasn't.* People didn't need me to be brilliant or beautiful or an expert. They needed to see Jesus in me. Then, *He would make the difference.*

When the Council saw the boldness of Peter and John, and could see they were obviously uneducated, non-professionals, they were amazed and realized what being with Jesus had done for them *(Acts 4:13 LB, emphasis mine).*

The rain was so heavy it was hard to see through my car windshield. I jumped out of the car and ran into the service station just off the Oklahoma interstate. "Hi. I know you have people outside waiting for you. Just wanted to tell you God loves you. He can give your life the meaning you're searching for."

The attendant froze. Tears welled up in his eyes. I gave him the last Bible.

To You, O Lord, I lift up my soul; in You I trust, O my God (Ps. 25:1 NIV).

Keep your eyes on Jesus, our leader and instructor. . . .
For all God's words are right,
and everything He does is worthy of our trust.

I pray that you will begin to understand how incredibly great
His power is to help those who believe Him.
It is that same mighty power that raised Christ from the dead.

Assign me Godliness and Integrity as my bodyguards,
for I expect you to protect me.

God loves you very much . . . don't be afraid!
Calm yourself; be strong . . .
Comfort those who are frightened;
take tender care of those who are weak.

He surrounds me with lovingkindness and tender mercies. . . .
Just as the mountains surround and protect Jerusalem,
so the Lord surrounds and protects His people.

I will lie down in peace and sleep, for though I am alone,
O Lord, You will keep me safe.

(Heb. 12:2; Ps. 33:4; Eph. 1:19; Ps. 25:21; Dan. 10:19; 1 Thess.
5:14; Ps. 103:4; 125:2; Ps. 4:8 LB).

Part 3.

God Makes the Difference In Our Obedience

WE GLANCE AT OUR FAILINGS,
DEVISE EXCUSES TO HIDE OUR GUILT,
AND HURRY ON BY . . .

WE HOPE GOD WON'T NOTICE,
AND WILL MAKE A DIFFERENCE *ANYWAY*.

Chapter 8.

But It's Such a Good Excuse!

We can always "prove" that we are right,
but is the Lord convinced? (Prov. 16:2 LB).

==

I'd like to return this, please." I handed the sack containing the blouse to the saleslady who had sold it to me the day before.

While visiting friends outside Chicago, I had met some college kids who needed Bibles and I was just a little short of having enough money to buy them. If I added the money from my blouse, I'd be able to get a Bible for each one.

"I can't accept this," said the saleslady as she showed me a soiled spot on the sleeve.

"It must have been there when I bought it," I explained. "You can see I've never worn it . . . the tags are still on it. I haven't even had it out of the sack."

"That doesn't matter. It's company policy."

"All right," I said glumly.

"I'm sorry."

"That's all right." The words were okay, but my tone was sour.

As I drove out of the store's parking lot, I felt God reproving me,

You were a terrific witness for Me just now.

Don't hassle me, God. I didn't say anything wrong.

Your spirit was wrong.

God, it was okay! Besides, look what I was returning the blouse for—Bibles for college kids! Just leave me alone!

So He did!

I drove in silence. No . . . more than silence. I felt alone. Gradually, there were echoes of past conversations.

You *decide what kind of Christian you're going to be,* God had told me. *I give you My name, My love, My help. You must also accept My disciplines. It's the only way you can be all I created you to be.* You *decide.*

God . . . You don't really want me to go back and apologize, do You?

Silence.

She probably didn't even notice.

Silence.

I'll bet I was nice compared to the way most people act.

I was sorry I'd said that. God had told me the world wasn't to be my standard; instead, His holiness was to be the standard for my life.

Do not model yourselves on the behavior of the world around you, but let your behavior change, modeled by your new mind. This is the only way to discover the will of God (Rom. 12:2, JB).

Life's crowded schedule . . . or is it simply the process of living . . . erodes the time intended for fellowship with God.
There's no time
   to personally apply Jesus' words.
There's no time
   to get close enough to God to hear His whispers.
There's no time
   for God to show us His next step for us.

We hurriedly read God's instructions about how to live ... accept them, feel inspired by them, affirm them as truth.

Then, we walk away,
    no different than we were before.

When something, someone ... even God ... reminds us of Jesus' instructions for our lives ... we feel a need to justify. To explain away. To present footnoted excuses for our failings.

We point to our past
    our future
    our present.
We dredge up resumés of our parents
        our mates
        our children
        our friends
        our pastor.

"Look at this! Look at them! How can you expect something else from me?" we exclaim, hiding in our alibi-cushioned boxes.

It doesn't happen by osmosis ... this becoming what God wants us to be. It doesn't happen by just reading Scriptures. Or by keeping the Bible near our favorite chair like a lucky charm.

We are not magically transformed into the Christians we need to be when we reach the age of 21 or 33 or 65. Nor when we become successful in our vocation. Nor when we have settled our family in a new home.

We *decide* ... you and I ... if we will let God make the difference in our lives. We decide what kind of Christians we will be.

That's no fun, is it? Being so responsible for the depth of our relationship with God.

Some of us established a pattern of *not* taking responsibility for our actions and reactions when we were very young:

Old enough to understand and obey, a child breaks a dish he has been told repeatedly not to touch.

Inevitably, someone chides the parent, "You shouldn't keep nice things around to tempt children."

A youngster hits his brother.

"He shouldn't have made fun of me!"

Then, we graduate to grown-up excuses:

Someone is rude to a waitress.

"Well, I gave her my order *twice*. What do you expect?"

A wife gives her husband the silent treatment.

"It serves him right! He never talks anything over with me, anyway."

A husband slams the door at his wife as he leaves for work.

"She deserved it! I'm sick of her nagging. Maybe it will teach her a lesson."

We harbor bitterness; nurse wounds.

Well, anyone would admit we were truly wronged.

We aren't developing our fellowship with God.

Just as soon as our business gets rolling. Or this project is over. Or the kids are a little older. Or our finances get straightened out . . . *then* we'll become the Christians we should be.

Perhaps that's one reason we clutch our boxes so tightly. They are our notarized affidavits that everything we do that's wrong . . . everything we should do—but don't . . . is the fault of something or someone else.

But, we don't live our lives in little compartments. It just doesn't work that way. We can't dump responsibility for ourselves on people or circumstances . . . then come to God openly, honestly, with no excuses.

No, we continue that same pattern with God. Sometimes we spend so much time justifying what we *aren't*, we have very little time and energy left to work on what we *are*.

Help me love Your every wish; then I will never have to be ashamed of myself (Ps. 119:80 LB).

You and I are not responsible for everything that happens. But we *are* responsible for what we do with what happens. We may not respond to circumstances in the same way others do; we may need a different kind of help from God than our friends. But, *we* still must decide . . .

> if we will give God the freedom to help us.
> if we will follow His instructions.
> if we will let *God make the difference.*

We ask too much of God. We ask Him to jump hurdles over our un-Christlike behavior, our un-Christlike words, and our priorities that are not Christ-centered.

How can we walk together with your sins between us? (Amos 3:3 LB).

It's not that big a deal, God. Lots *of people do it.*

How can we walk together with your sins between us?

Now, God . . . I'm doing everything else *you want me to. Don't bug me about this one area, this one thing.*

How can we walk together . . . ?

God, I'm living a lot better life than most people I know.

We don't usually use that last argument out loud, for then we'd really have to *look* at it . . . and it would look pretty shabby. But, tucked away in our thoughts, we can call on it to quickly gloss over lots of things. It's very effective.

There's even a Scripture to back it up. You know, the one that says,

The world is your standard. As long as you're doing better than those who aren't Christians, you're living exactly as I wish, saith the Lord.

Well, I say there's a Scripture like that . . . surely there must be. Actually, I've been unable to find it, but I'm probably using the wrong translation.

Or could it be
   that our *Pure* God,
   our *Holy* God,
   won't take part in our games?

How can we walk together?

God does the work in our hearts and minds; He is the One Who wants to create His own likeness in us. But *we* decide . . . you and I . . . whether we give Him the freedom to accomplish that work. We decide if we will drop the excuses and face God with just . . . ourselves.

Let us throw off everything that hinders . . . Let us fix our eyes on Jesus (Heb. 12:1, 2 NIV).

I turned the car around and drove back to the store.

I hoped that, since this was what God wanted, the doors of the store would swing open as I approached, that people would form an easily accessible path to the clerk, and that she'd be expecting me.

Not so. I waited what seemed like an hour, but was probably only ten minutes before the saleslady who had helped me was free.

"I want to ask your forgiveness for the way I acted a few minutes ago," I said.

"You didn't do anything wrong." She looked bewildered.

"My spirit was wrong. I want to be a better person than that. I wronged you and I'm so sorry. Please forgive me."

She did. I walked away even more ashamed. She never asked why I apologized, so I had no opportunity to share with her about

God. My actions had forfeited that right. What could I say? "Lady, I'm a Christian . . . I just don't *act* like one!"

This time as I drove away, I prayed, *Thank You, God, for not letting me get away with a bad attitude.*

I was learning that each excuse I give for my un-Christlike behavior makes the next excuse easier.

Listening to God isn't always easy.

Obedience isn't always painless.

What happiness for those whose guilt has been forgiven! . . . What relief for those who have confessed their sins and God has cleared their record (Ps. 32:1, 2 LB).

Chapter 9.

I Almost *Always* Obey God

For God is at work within you, helping
you want to obey him, and then helping
you do what he wants (Phil. 2:13 LB).

I woke up startled! Immediately I thought of Mrs. Graystone. This elderly lady had thick snowy hair and a smile that hugged you.

I felt God saying to me:

She's dying and she feels alone. I want you to go be with her. Now.

I held my little clock with florescent hands close so I could see the time without putting on my glasses. Three o'clock in the morning! *God, I barely know her,* I pled. *She might not even know who I am. . . .*

As I put the clock down, I dismissed as irrelevant the fact that I remembered which hospital she was in. *It's so late,* I thought as I pulled up the covers. *It can wait till morning. . . . It probably wasn't God, anyway.* And I went back to sleep.

The next morning, I called the hospital to check on Mrs. Graystone. She had died at five o'clock that morning . . . alone.

I was shaken. There was no way to make that up. Not to Mrs. Graystone. Not to God.

It scared me to think how easily, how casually I'd dismissed what God had told me to do. How noncommittal I'd been about His directions. How often did I do that?

Why do you keep calling me, "Lord, Lord"—and never do what I tell you? (Luke 6:46 NEB).

I remembered when God had said to me,

My children want Me to give them a plan to change the whole world, then they'll be obedient. But they don't have the time to obey what they consider a small assignment. You must be faithful with the seemingly small tasks before you will hear My voice clearly enough to be trusted with other responsibilities.

So I had been trying to respond to thoughts which I'd never before considered God's leading—impulses to write a note, phone a friend, pray for whomever came to my mind.

As a toddler's legs become stronger with each new step . . . as a driver sees farther down the road around each new curve . . . I found that the more I acted on those inner promptings, the more of God's direction I received.

But how often had I been glib about the timing, fitting the "obedience" into *my* schedule? I wondered . . . was *late* obedience really obedience at all?

I searched through the Scriptures, studying every verse on obedience. I'd never noticed before that each of God's promises was linked to an obedient response. I tended to skip the obedience part and get right to the promised reward. I wanted God to do all that good stuff for me without having to fulfill His requirements.

I couldn't let this slide any longer. *God, help me understand the imperative of obeying You.*

Now try with every fiber of your being to obey the Lord your God (1 Chron. 22:19 LB).

During a church committee meeting, the Minister of Christian Education mentioned Professor Bob Verl. "He's so talented," Keith said, "and the college kids love him."

The moment Keith mentioned Professor Verl's name, from somewhere deep inside . . . as clearly as if the words were spoken aloud . . . I heard,

I'm going to perform a miracle for Bob.

In that same moment, I believed it was God speaking to me. That night in my devotions I prayed for Professor Verl.

I'm going to heal him.

The same almost-audible impression. Again I believed it was God's voice and that He meant what He said. I was excited and began praying for Professor Verl's healing.

I want you to tell him.

Tell him what? I asked God, not wanting to hear the answer.

Tell him I'm going to heal him.

God, I think it's great You're going to heal him. Feel free to go right ahead and do it. I'll be glad to pray for him, but that's all!

I want you to tell him.

God, I don't even know the man. I don't know what's wrong with him. I've never done anything like that before. You *tell him.*

Pretending I'd never heard God's instructions didn't work. They echoed in my thoughts.

God, I don't understand what's going on, I pleaded. *But it's scary. I'm not ready for this.*

Glaphré, do you realize how often you do this to me? I felt God saying.

God was right. He and I seemed to repeat the same old struggle.

He'd direct,
 and I'd resist.
  Always for the same reason . . .
   What God wanted didn't fit *me.*
   I couldn't do it.

I thought I'd gotten rid of my box. Oh, maybe the lid was gone, maybe even a couple of sides. No . . . I'd really given the entire box to God. But I knew exactly where all its boundaries had been . . . and a lot of the time I stayed inside those boundaries.

Why won't you believe more in what I *can do than in what* you *can't do? Why do you listen more to your own fears than to My instructions? Why do you look at* you? LOOK AT ME! OBEY ME!

You must obey all *the commandments of the Lord your God, following His directions in every detail,* going the whole way He has laid out for you *(Deut. 5:32 LB, emphasis mine).*

A few days later I saw Keith and tried to ask casually, "How's Bob Verl doing? Is he feeling okay?"

"He's doing great!" Keith answered with his usual enthusiasm. "No problems I'm aware of."

That's terrific, God! I thought. *You want to heal someone who isn't even sick! See what a mess I almost made! I have this message all mixed up, haven't I?*

I was frightened and hoped that would be the end of it.

On *Thursday* morning of that same week, I woke up with a strong feeling that I should go to Professor Verl's house and tell him God's message . . . but I didn't.

On *Saturday* afternoon I took a drive and stopped at a small, brown field punctuated by telephone poles. I climbed through the broken wire fence and sat on a piece of old log. It was one of those special times with God when He shared things I needed to work on . . . things I needed to learn.

As I stood to leave, I felt God saying,

Look to the right.

To the right was the only patch of green in this barren dirt field.

That's Bob. Alive. Healthy. Well. And you're to tell him.

God, please give me a Scripture verse to help me know this is You, and not some crazy thing I've come up with on my own.

I opened my Bible and read:

"I have seen the Lord!" Then she gave them His message (John 20:18 LB).

I struggled through the evening. Finally, I typed a letter.

Dear Professor Verl:
You don't know me. My dad is your pastor. I don't know what's wrong with you, sir, but I believe you're sick . . .

I prayed over the letter, partly for help . . . but mostly to postpone what now seemed inevitable. Just before midnight, I looked up the address in the phone book. Still nervous, I got into my car and looked for a service station for directions to Professor Verl's house. No service station was open.

I wanted to go home, but I drove to the general vicinity of his address and stopped. *God, I know if I'd been obedient Thursday when You directed, or even this afternoon, I could have asked someone how to get here—service stations would have been open, my parents would have been awake. This is late obedience . . . but I am trying. Please help!*

I can't explain how I knew where to turn right, when to turn left. There was never a turn I was truly confident of. It just seemed each time that this *might* be the right corner. Finally . . . there was the street. I stopped every few houses and nervously checked the numbers in the darkness of early morning. At last I found the Verls' house. I weakly thanked God for His direction. . . My stomach felt like I was on a roller coaster as I slipped the letter into the mailbox.

I am the Lord . . . who confirms the word of his servant and performs the counsel of his messengers (Isa. 44:24, 26 RSV).

"Glaphré, you have a phone call." As Mom handed me the phone, she whispered, "I think the man is crying."

"I'm Bob Verl and I just got your letter." His voice was trembling. "I want to tell you something in confidence. A few weeks ago I found out I might be dying. The test results aren't good, and this week the pain has been so much worse. It's a bad sign. I go to the hospital tomorrow for more tests, but the doctor has told us it doesn't look good."

I sat there listening to Professor Verl . . . almost in disbelief.

"I don't know when your letter came," he continued. "*Thursday* was the only day last week we were home. My wife and I have been at our cabin trying to accept whatever is ahead, and trying to figure out how to tell our boys. The pain was much more severe on Thursday . . . but it stopped *Saturday night*. I haven't had any pain since."

I cried silently as I listened to Professor Verl. Why hadn't I been obedient? How could I be so selfish?

"Your letter was such a help to me," he continued. "To think God loves me enough to have someone pray for me. It has helped me remember God knows what is happening. Whatever happens, I know God cares."

First, I asked his forgiveness for my lack of obedience on

Thursday. Then I said, "I don't know what kind of illness you've had, but the tests will be clear." My voice was calm and confident. It reflected the way I felt.

God touched Professor Verl. The tests showed an absence of any disease.

So they cried to the Lord in their distress . . . he brought them out of darkness, dark as death. . . . Let them thank the Lord for His enduring love (Ps. 107:13–15 NEB).

It's not a single act of obedience that makes the difference. We're not to obey once . . . and then eagerly look around for the result. We can't carry out God's desires a couple of times, then stand back and exclaim:

Look what *I* did God.
   Now, it's Your turn . . .
      make a difference!

We have to build obedience on top of obedience . . . until it becomes a way of life. Only then do we experience the fullness and constancy of God's presence.

God makes the difference.
   But we decide . . . you and I . . .
      if we will let Him.

Jesus replied, "Because I will only reveal myself to those who love Me and obey Me (John 14:23 LB).

Who may climb the mountain of the Lord
and enter where He lives?
Who may stand before the Lord?

Only those with pure hands and hearts,
who do not practice dishonesty and lying.
They will receive God's own goodness as their blessing from Him,
planted in their lives by God Himself, their Savior.

These are the ones who are allowed to stand
before the Lord and worship
the God of Jacob.   (Ps. 24:3–6, LB).

Part 4.

God Makes the Difference In Our Hurt

WE LOOK AT OUR LIVES,
CRIPPLED BY THE SCRAPS OF OUR PAST,
BOUND BY NEGATIVE CIRCUMSTANCES,
WOUNDED BY THOSE WE TRUSTED . . .
EVEN GOD.

GOD COULD NEVER
MAKE A DIFFERENCE *HERE*.

Chapter 10.

The Formulas Don't Always Work

I cry to the Lord . . . I am in deep
trouble and I need his help so badly (Ps. 77:1–2 LB).

We live in a world of instant solutions. All of life's problems
from loneliness to self-acceptance to troubled family relationships
can be solved within the span of a one-minute commercial.

Given our natural human resistance to discipline, when we
have a problem, we expect God to hand down *our* prescribed
answer easily, immediately, just the way we ordered it.

We're encouraged by many popular spiritual formulas that
promise quick and effortless results. Their proponents are positive the formulas work, validating them by true stories and Scriptures that say we can have anything we want.

Decide what you want.
Tell God.
Believe hard.
And it's yours!

It sounds great! Having God as our errand boy is almost as
good as having an ever-ready Santa Claus.

Sometimes the formulas work wonderfully well! And it's very
exciting.

But what about the times we pray for something . . . I mean *really believing* . . . and nothing seems to happen? What do we do with the spiritual formulas then?

The formula-givers usually interpret lack of results by saying: "That person wasn't believing hard enough," or, "That person is hiding some secret sin." Pointing to the miracles of others, they proclaim, "You see?"

The insincere heart dismisses these explanations. It's the sincere heart that is affected. We beat ourselves on the heads for being the only Christians around without total success, and our discouraged, heavy spirits begin to smother our faith. Or, we force optimism and try again.

The problem is . . . the formulas don't always work. The very people who insist they do either have not yet experienced personal trauma, or are denying the difficulties in their own lives. Often the very ones who insist God has great financial wealth for all of His children are pleading desperately for our financial contributions in order that their ministries might survive. They seem to see no inconsistency there.

Despite all we hear to the contrary, regardless of how much we wish it were true . . .

life is not a neat package
    that never comes unraveled
        if you're a Christian.

Using today's popular formulas, how do we interpret the life of the Apostle Paul? In 2 Corinthians, Paul prayed three times for the removal of affliction and God said, "My grace is sufficient for thee" (12:9).

There's a lot of debate about the nature of Paul's thorn. Does it matter? Is one thorn more or less spiritual than another? Isn't what matters that, whatever the thorn, Paul sought deliverance . . . but got grace instead?

Some people might argue that Paul didn't believe *hard* enough. Using the success formulas, we'd also be forced to interpret his

Christian life as a failure. After all, Paul's ministry was reduced to writing letters from prison.

And how would we interpret Jesus' life? Deserted by friends . . . publicly ridiculed . . . a Man of Sorrows and acquainted with grief. . . .

In the midst of the discussion and clatter, surely the formulas would compel us to conclude that there must be things about Him we don't know. For if He had experienced any *real* faith, everything in His life would have been different.

We'd probably cancel His message of peace, His offer to make a difference in us, and His instruction to follow Him. We'd leave Him and go look for a leader who espoused a more "comfortable" approach to life.

A dangerous exchange—this switching roles with God. This belief that God must act on *our* conclusions of what is best and needed. This requiring God to fulfill *our* desires *our* way.

What happens when God doesn't jump through the hoop we hold up? Especially when hoop-jumping and errand-hopping is the only kind of help we want from God.

For I have come here from heaven to do the will of God who sent me, not to have my own way *(John 6:38 LB, emphasis mine).*

When Ellie discovered I was in a nearby town, she called to see if she could drive over for a while. It was fun having a catch-up time with a friend I hadn't seen in several years. As Ellie proudly displayed pictures of her grandchildren, I thought, *She's still the same caring person.*

But when she called, Ellie hadn't said she wanted to "visit." She had asked for an "appointment."

"You have something on your mind, don't you?" I asked.

"Glaphré, I've got to get some help." Ellie told me of a bout with depression she had just worked through with the help of her family and Christian counseling.

"I have been doing fine, and feeling all right about the experience until recently," she continued. "But the people in my prayer group keep telling me if I were a good enough Christian, I never would have had this trouble."

Ellie wiped her tears with the back of her hand, "I didn't mean to let God down. You know how important it is to me to be the person God wants me to be."

"Could I ask you some questions about your group?" I asked, handing her a Kleenex. "Does anyone in your prayer group have problems in business or with finances?"

Ellie nodded.

"Are there any family or marital problems among the members of your group?"

"Well, yes," she admitted. "But I don't see what that has to do with my depression."

"Are those people considered 'lesser' Christians because of their problems?"

"No," she answered, catching on.

"Who decides, Ellie, which problems are okay to have and still be classified a 'good Christian'? Isn't what matters that, whatever our problem, God has help for us? Sometimes He gives deliverance. Sometimes He gives grace. But He always makes a difference."

We talked and prayed and God gave her release.

The good man does not escape all troubles—he has them too. But the Lord helps him in each and every one (Ps. 34:19 LB).

When you have a problem you can't seem
   to pray away . . .
When the circumstances are so dark, you can't see
   what to do . . .
When the formulas aren't working . . .
   Forget the formulas.
Release to God the judgment of the formula-givers
   and look to God.
He will make the difference.

Looking unto Jesus the Author *and finisher of our faith (Heb. 12:2 KJV).*

Chapter 11.

When the Unthinkable Happens

We expected peace, but no peace came;
we looked for health but there was only
terror (Jer. 8:15 LB).

*W*hen they opened the door for me, the large dark-paneled room seemed crowded. Not because of the medical research team who greeted me, but because of the heaviness of their mood . . . it was almost suffocating.

The doctor behind the desk looked through my chart, explaining the results of recent medical tests. I couldn't even pronounce the words he was using . . . I'd never heard some of them before. Though I didn't understand the words, I did understand his somber tone.

I looked around the room at the physicians sitting in their black-tufted leather chairs. The grim expressions on their faces spoke more loudly than the explanation I was receiving.

Strange that the room seemed crowded. Now each new statement stripped the room, leaving only the frightening words . . . *bedridden . . . deformed . . . We don't know how much time you have left . . . We're sorry, there's nothing we can do.*

The room felt cold.

And I felt alone.

"Glaphré, this condition you were born with is extremely rare. You know that we've been very surprised at the quality of life you've had so far. But we thought it necessary to acquaint you with this approaching stage of the illness. Do you have any questions?"

I guess I should have had a lot of questions, but I couldn't think of any.

"Glaphré," he said as he stood, "we want you to be as prepared as possible for what is ahead of you. I'm afraid it's going to get rough."

I was led to a long library table filled with medical books, open to photographs of people grossly deformed by the final stages of this illness. As I walked the length of the table, I no longer heard any of the comments. These men seemed to be unaware that a part of me was dying . . . a crucial, intimate part. As they closed the last book, I felt my future and my happiness closing with it.

I didn't understand enough to know that the awful hurt I felt was grief. I had heard a lot about what happens to a person who loses a mate or a parent or a child. But I didn't know that the same process takes place when you lose a part of yourself.

It wasn't anything tangible like an eye or a leg.
    It was just
        . . . all my dreams
        . . . all my hopes.

I never knew they had occupied such a big part of my life but their absence left a crushing darkness.

What do you do when a part of you is dying?
    Conduct a funeral?
Call your friends in and announce
    "I'm only part of a person now"?
Where's the bandage for that kind of hurt?

I don't remember leaving the medical building . . . or finding my car . . . or driving home. I hid for a few days, not going to church or work or accepting social engagements. After that I only hid "inside," retreating into my box.

The people around me never suspected, for I threw myself feverishly into activities. At church I taught a Sunday school class, directed a teen choir, sang in the adult choir, served on committees. As a new Junior High teacher of chorus and drama, I rehearsed long hours with the kids, from early morning into the night hours.

The frantic activity was a desperate attempt to fill the emptiness. To salve the hurt.

When that didn't work, I tried to fill the inner void with daydreaming—drowning reality in fantasies filled with happy scenes of my home, my own family. Seeing myself happy, healthy, full of energy, helping others.

There is a problem with trying to fill an emptiness inside with anything except what is supposed to be there. Just as with alcoholism or drug addiction, you have to return more and more often to your chosen source of escape to get the same amount of relief. I'm not saying there's no relief. Just that it doesn't last for very long.

The clamor of the alarm clock reminded me that it was time to get dressed for church. I'd already been awake for quite a while . . . keeping busy trying not to think about *me*.

"Honey, it's time to get up," Mom called cheerfully when she walked by my room. As I had grown weaker, I was no longer able to maintain my own apartment, so I had moved in with my family. And more and more often Mom had to drive me to school and church functions.

I didn't *want* to get up. I hated getting dressed! It was one of the most vivid reminders of what was happening to me. I couldn't wear the styles or sizes I was used to and special adjustments had to be made to hide the beginning deformities. It didn't matter that most of the changes in my body could still be covered by clothing . . . *I* knew they were there.

Each new development exhumed those terrifying medical pictures. Every physical change unleashed fears of being trapped.

Never being happy.
  Never being fulfilled.
    Never being useful.

Waiting until the last possible minute, I dragged myself out of bed, just far enough to sit on the end of it. I didn't want to get dressed.

I'm glad Mom knows how to sew, I thought, looking at my closet. *I couldn't take shopping anymore.*

I shuddered as I recalled recent encounters with salesclerks.

"Our dresses don't come in sizes that large," one would say loudly enough to be heard by nearby shoppers. *Why couldn't she at least have whispered?*

Or a saleslady would open the dressing room curtain as she asked cheerfully, "How are we coming? Does it fit?"

Of course it doesn't fit! Nothing fits! I don't want you looking at me! I don't want anyone looking at me! I screamed inwardly. But I answered in a quiet, deliberate tone, "I can't tell yet. I'll let you know."

"Would you like me to zip you?" she'd ask, smiling.

How can she be so pleasant? How can she act like the world is normal? Why doesn't she get out of here! I don't want her or anyone else touching me! But what I said aloud was a polite, 'No, thank you."

The next time I needed clothes, I came home from school to find several dresses lying on my bed. Mom had sensed my hurt and had done the shopping without me. I made selections in the privacy of my room, and she took the other garments back. What didn't fit, she altered. No fuss. No big deal. She didn't make a production out of it.

It wasn't because I had told her of my struggle. Though my family and a close friend knew most of what the doctors had said,

I couldn't tell them what I felt inside. I was trying too hard to pretend everything was okay. Talking about it would have made it . . . real.

After church that Sunday, my brother Ron brought ten of his college friends home for Sunday lunch. Mom fed and mothered them. Dad answered their questions about life and encouraged their belief in themselves and their future. Our family always lingered at the table. Warm, laughing, loving moments.

I couldn't relate to the stories I heard about the trials of being reared in a minister's home. I had memories of . . .

Family softball games and corporate aerial attempts with our kites on windy afternoons.
Dad leaving an important meeting to fly across the country to surprise me at my high-school play, even though he had to return right after I finished my part. I cried when I saw him there, but had no idea of the financial sacrifice it represented.
Mom listening far into the nights, hearing itemized accounts of each of our activities and feelings.
Dad's encouragement to dream dreams and not be afraid of failure.
Our parents praying for us before games, tests, choir tours, or new beginnings.

Though my parents' counsel was wise, the example of their lives spoke even more clearly about the meaning of the Christian life.

I'd heard that our concept of God is formed by our relationship with our parents and the preaching or teaching we hear. I had a tremendous headstart for, through my background, I knew God to be loving, tender, present, enabling, and forgiving.

What I didn't know was that *inner hurt and unfilled needs can distort even a positive concept of God.*

Looking at our Sunday lunch table crowded with Ron's friends, I thought about all the people who had found love and support in our family. The love was still there, but I couldn't allow it to get close enough to make any difference in my hurt.

After lunch, I went back to my room and began reading my Bible. A daily devotional time had been a fairly consistent part of my life since I was thirteen. And although right after my medical diagnosis I had continued my devotions out of habit, now my times with God were becoming more meaningful.

Spending more time with God was inconsistent with my response to the situation, wasn't it? But that's what I was— inconsistent. I'd commit the whole thing to God and really mean it. And I'd leave it with God for . . . oh . . . sometimes as long as four or five minutes.

Since I didn't seem to get anywhere in my prayers for healing, I longed for another kind of relief. Suicide was out. I figured God wouldn't be too thrilled with that. I wanted to go to heaven, but I wanted an immediate departure. It seemed like a fair request, and oh so much easier than delaying it and having to live with this thing.

These times in God's Word were my only solace.

Whom have I in heaven but You? And I desire no one on earth as much as You! My health fails; my spirits droop, yet God remains! In my distress I screamed to the Lord for His help. And He heard me from heaven (Ps. 73:25, 26; Ps. 18:6 LB).

I went into the kitchen to make a phone call and witnessed a familiar scene: Mom and Ron wrestling playfully in the den. Ron's college friends had formed a cheering section for Mom. They needn't have worried. Even though my brother was 6'3½'', Mom got him so tickled that she always won.

Their fun made me feel alone.

Pity me, O Lord, for I am weak. Heal me for my body is sick. . . . "You are my Lord; I have no other help but Yours. . . ." I am completely discouraged—I lie in the dust. Revive me by Your Word (Ps. 6:2; 16:2; 119:25 LB).

Chapter 12.

God, Do You Love Me Enough?

My only hope is in Your love (Ps. 40:11 LB).

*I*t was two in the morning and I couldn't sleep. The moon outside my bedroom window looked even brighter than the street lights. My parents were enjoying their new pastorate here in Oklahoma. And even though I hadn't been able to get out enough to become acclimated, I loved watching the star-filled nights through my curtains.

During these days in bed, the Bible, more than ever, had become my faithful companion. I looked down at my open Bible, not understanding why I kept stumbling over Scriptures about God's love. While I was reading them, I felt better. But when I was through, I felt more alone than ever. I thought it was a dumb reaction, so I added it to the growing list of things I didn't want to deal with.

Most of the time it's easy to tell when we need to learn something:

When the lake smacks us in the face, we know something went wrong with our water-skiing technique.

A soggy crust tells us we need to make the quiche differently next time.

The hurt expression on someone's face indicates we weren't as considerate as we should have been.

But in the areas concerning what we believe, it's not always so easy to detect incomplete learning. And often we're already so convinced we know something that we dismiss any suggestions we may need to learn more about it.

God is love. We don't have any arguments with that. Of course He is! Everyone knows that. That's an easy one . . . or is it?

Oh, we can locate the Scriptures that prove God's love. We even have a lot of them underlined in our Bibles. We sing beautiful songs about His love . . . songs that move us deeply. We tell people God loves them because we know it's true. We even teach Bible studies on God's love. Yes, we really know God loves us. Or do we?

God's Word tells how to evaluate what we believe about His love:

We need have no fear of someone who loves us perfectly; his perfect love for us eliminates all dread of what he might do to us. If we are afraid, it shows that we are not fully convinced he really loves us (1 John 4:18 LB, emphasis mine).

"If we are afraid" . . . not of God . . . but of what He will or won't do to help us. Fear . . . that could mean apprehension or anxiety or dread or panic. Rarely, when we have those feelings, do we recognize that we need God to reassure us that He loves us.

Maybe *last week* we knew He loved us. Maybe *next week* we'll know it again. Maybe we still strongly *believe* in God's love. But for *right now . . . in this circumstance . . .* we don't "feel" God's love. And we *need* to.

This loving Father we belong to . . . this gentle Shepherd Who has expressed His love for us in so many tender ways . . . this Holy Spirit Who is so available to us . . . is willing to reassure us of His love.

My only hope is in Your love and faithfulness. Otherwise I perish, for problems far too big for me to solve are piled higher than my head. . . . You

are my refuge and my shield, and Your promises are my only source of hope
(Ps. 40:11; 119:114 LB).

"Let Me teach you that I love you." That thought returned over and
over. And tonight I wasn't pushing it aside.

God, I don't know what You want. I can explain Your love to anyone; I
can teach a pretty good Sunday school lesson on it—I believe You love me.
So, what's the deal?

Be able to feel and understand . . . how deep . . . His love really is; and to
experience this love for yourselves (Eph. 3:18, 19 LB).

> *God, how could I* not *know You love me?*
> *You share Jesus with me.*
> *You forgive my sins.*
> *You open Your Word to me.*
> *You give me supportive friends and a loving family.*
> *You gave me tremendous opportunities when I was able*
> *to work.*
> *I* know *You're loving.*

My declaration sounded shaky . . . even to me. God was pro-
bing. What I wanted to believe didn't match what I felt.

Tears slid off my face and hit the pages of my Bible. From
somewhere deep within surfaced feelings I hadn't even admitted
to myself.

If You are so powerful and love me so much, God, then why aren't You
doing *something? Either heal me or let me die now. After all, I'm not being*
hard to get along with. I'm even giving You a choice!

Slowly, I began to see I had come to a destructive conclusion:

Not that God wasn't powerful.
　　Not that He didn't love me.
　　　　But that He didn't love me *enough*.
　　　　　　He didn't love me as much as I
　　　　　　　needed Him to. Not enough to help me.

It was difficult to admit ... even to myself. It was more difficult to admit to God.

I looked down at my Bible.

I have loved thee with an everlasting love (Jer. 31:3 KJV).

They were only *words*. An empty statement that meant nothing, for it didn't translate into tangible help.

Embarrassed by my thoughts, I confessed, *God, I don't believe You mean these promises of love. Not for me, at least. For salvation, yes. But not enough to do anything about the horrible circumstances of my life.*

Gradually, God led me to pray a prayer that was to change my life: *God, teach me that You love me.*

When I felt lonely:
  God, teach me that You love me.
While I was brushing my teeth:
  God, teach me that You love me.
As I was falling asleep:
  God, teach me that You love me.

The darkness within ... unable to remain in the presence of hope ... began to creep away ... *God, teach me that You love me.*

It didn't happen in a day. But gradually I became aware of God's continuing, loving presence. It helped me feel safe, even with my hurt.

I had wanted God to change my circumstances. Instead, God's love was changing *me*.

I will rejoice and be glad in Thy unfailing love; for Thou hast seen my affliction and hast cared for me in my distress. Thou hast not abandoned me (Ps. 31:7, 8 NEB).

Every once in a while, my young nieces will crawl up into their daddy's lap and say, "I want a hug!"

When she was growing up, it wasn't unusual for my sister to pop a question into the middle of a family conversation: "Do you love me, huh?" The question was always accompanied by a smile. It wasn't that Sheri didn't know. It was that she liked hearing the words.

When we need God to help us feel His love . . . *He will.* We don't need to be ashamed or embarrassed or think we should have grown "beyond" needing His reassurance. *God is love.* And since He is . . . don't you think He's happy to help us feel it?

There is a prayer that can change your life. It is simply this: *God, teach me that You love me.*

Wherever we are in our Christian growth . . . whatever our present circumstances . . . this prayer frees us to believe in God's love more than our problems.

God, teach me that You love me.

Let Thy unfailing love, O Lord, rest upon us, as we have put our hope in Thee. . . . This one thing I know: God is for me! (Ps. 33:22 NEB; Ps. 56:9 LB).

Chapter 13.

Nothing Is Wasted

"Now gather the scraps," Jesus told
His disciples (John 6:12 LB).

*R*eminders of civilization were hidden in this quiet place. Tall
trees bordered the field across the road, shutting out the world. I
smiled as I looked at the red dirt of the road. Visitors to Oklahoma were always surprised by its colorful earth.

Reclining on a lounge chair on the porch of my parents' cabin,
I watched the ever-present Oklahoma wind rearranging the dry
soil. The field across from the cabin was clouded in a pale red
haze of dust. I was enjoying my few days alone here.

I looked down at my Bible and read the verse one more time,
trying to understand what God wanted to tell me.

*"Now gather the scraps," Jesus told his disciples, "so that nothing is
wasted" (John 6:12 LB).*

*God, I'm really glad Jesus wasn't a litterbug, but I still don't see any
great spiritual significance in this verse.*

I felt God saying to me:

You won't do that with Me, Glaphré.
You won't give Me the scraps.
You want Me to make them go away.
But that's not the way I work.

I don't throw the scraps away.
I don't waste the hurt.
I heal *it.*
I want more for you than a life of
   semi-fulfillment.
      I want you to be whole.

God was right. I did want Him to make the scraps disappear. I was tired of feeling lousy, of looking lousy. But I didn't want *help* with my hurt . . . I wanted to be *well!* It would be so easy for God to do.

My condition had progressed more slowly than predicted. After I had to resign my teaching position, there were still times when I had the strength to do something. The year I traveled, although I spent the majority of my time in bed, God miraculously provided His strength for His ministry.

At every critical moment . . . when the doctors were the most gloomy . . . when I was too weak to even turn over in bed . . . when the pain was too great to take any more . . . God intervened and granted me a reprieve. Until the next time.

I couldn't understand why He didn't just heal me completely—once and for all. It seemed a better conservation of His energy. It would take a burst of creative power, but then He'd be all done and wouldn't have to mess with it anymore.

I wanted relief of some kind so much . . . healing or death . . . that sometimes I was not even grateful for the miraculous help God did give.

"God, I'm sorry," I cried out, "I don't want You to *heal* the scraps. I want You to make them *disappear!*"

A very understanding God responded,

If your happiness . . . your fulfillment . . . is so tied to outward circumstances, what happens when the circumstances change? Is the fulfillment gone again?

I thought of how often a side or two of my box reappeared to cover the aching inside. But I had never admitted, even to myself, that I had left my hurt, my scraps inside the protective custody of my box.

I had dreamed of a day when God would swoop down and annihilate my goblins, correct all my problems, fight off death . . . and heal my physical condition. My scraps would disintegrate, never to return, because I was well. *Then,* I'd be ready to face the world. *Then,* life would be fulfilling.

I'd never considered having to face the world and life with circumstances unresolved, with the future growing dimmer every day. I was wanting God to change my circumstances. God was wanting to change *me*.

God was so patient.

Glaphré, what you become doesn't have to be decided by what you look like, or how you feel, or by any other circumstance. Your life can be expressed by My abundance.

All these years . . . how had I missed it? I was believing the negatives of life would destroy my happiness, my usefulness, more than I believed God's love and power would preserve it.

In a dark medical conference room, I'd taken part of my attention off God and focused instead on medical pictures. On a medical prognosis. On my fears. In the lonely days that followed, I decided God's responsibility was to make me well. To make all my dreams come true. And He wasn't doing that!

I had allowed those negative circumstances to reshape my feelings about myself and cripple my approach to life.

I'd made a commitment to belong to God completely. I guess that meant my hurt, too. I had assumed there were two choices: The emotional hurt could go away because of physical healing and the problem would therefore be resolved; or, I could learn to cope with my circumstances. God was now saying there was another choice.

Glaphré, you can trust Me with the scraps.

Finally,
   as a child tearfully brings
     the broken pieces of a favorite toy
      to his father,
I crawled into the box,
   gathered up my scraps,
     and gave them
      to God.

   I didn't know what to expect. I can't explain it, but God . . .
oh, so gently . . . took my thoughts back to damaging events and
with His tender love, He restructured them.

There was Jesus . . . in the doctors' conference room, standing at
the end of the library table filled with medical pictures. He took
my face in His hands and, with a tenderness I'll never forget,
said, *These pictures aren't a reflection of what you're going to become. I
AM. Look into My eyes. What you see there is what you will be.*

And . . . oh . . . the love I saw!
   The dismal room was illuminated with it.
   The monstrous pictures were transformed by it.

There was Jesus . . . sitting on the edge of my bed in the middle of
the night. Nights when I muffled my desperation with my pillow.
Nights when I longed to die. Nights when I felt abandoned.

Jesus wiped away the tears.
   Comforted the desperation.
   The nights were no longer cold and dark.

There was Jesus . . . sitting on the desks of all the doctors who said
there was no hope. He winked at me and said, *They don't know. I
AM your Hope.*

There was Jesus . . . standing with His arm around me as I looked into the mirror, sickened by my reflection.

You're looking at the wrong things, He said.
   He showed me Himself.

There was Jesus . . . gathering up my fantasies and dead dreams.

I have far better dreams for you, He encouraged.
   And He helped me believe it.

   It didn't just happen in my head or in my mind. It happened in my hurt. God's tender love was freeing me to see *Him* instead of what was wrong with me. There was no need for the box anymore. The scraps were gone.
   Tears slowly wet my face as I noticed the tumbleweeds bouncing alongside the cabin porch . . . *I* felt that free!

Daisy-like wildflowers accented the side of the cabin—
   Scattered bunches of gentle life.
The sky was bluer.
   The grass greener.
I was free! No more painful scraps from yesterday.
   I was whole! *Inside* I was healed.
I sat in God-hushed stillness . . .
   and, oh . . . the peace!

But for you who fear my name, the Sun of Righteousness will rise with healing in His wings. And you will go free, leaping with joy like calves let out to pasture (Mal. 4:2 LB).

Chapter 14.

Jesus Heals the Scraps

I will not leave you comfortless:
I will come to you (John 14:18 KJV).

I had tried to time it so I would always arrive at the car wash on Highway 66 when the place was empty. Today I'd made it! As I attempted to control the gadget spewing water on my car, I noticed Stan sitting by himself. Stan was the part-time operator of this self-help car wash.

After I finished spraying my car, I sat down on the bench by this small, seventy-six-year-old man who didn't shave or bathe very often.

"What's wrong, Stan?"

"Seeing you just reminded me, that's all," he mumbled, never looking up. "Must be nice to be so young and have all of life ahead of you."

"Stan, what do you wish were ahead of you?"

Still looking at his feet, he murmured so softly I barely understood him, "I don't know . . . some relief . . . God."

Stan shuffled his feet in the gravel. His worn-out shoes matched his overalls. There was such sadness in him as he told me about the scraps of his past. "I've heard all that stuff about God forgiving people. But He could *never* forgive all that I've done." His voice trembled with his anguished conclusion.

I knew how the scraps of our past could gouge our hopes for the future. But I knew something much more important—I knew God could heal scraps . . . because that's what He had done for me.

Secure in God's willingness to accept Stan's scraps, I asked, "Stan, do you know the story of what happened when Jesus was on the cross?"

He nodded, still staring at the ground. "Stan," I continued, "people yelled and screamed awful things at Jesus. Yet even as they were crucifying Him, He prayed, 'Father, forgive them; they don't know what they're doing.' Do you believe that really happened?"

"Oh, I believe the story of Jesus, all right."

"Stan, why don't you let God guide your thoughts for a minute. Think of the worst thing you ever did; you don't need to tell me what it is. . . . Can you think of it?"

"Yes, but I wish I could forget it."

"Stan," I asked, slipping my arm around him, "can you think of Jesus walking into that scene? With the same compassion He had at the cross, Jesus says to you: 'Stan, is this thing you're remembering worse than nailing Me to a cross? Than killing Me? If I could forgive that, won't I forgive you?'

"Stan, this loving and forgiving God has His arms open to you. God is pleading with you: 'I've waited for you such a long time. I want you for My very own son.'"

This little man, who was crumpled over with grief, sobbed out his acceptance to God.

A couple of cars pulled in and I went to move my car out of the way.

In the weeks that followed, the people at the car wash were surprised by Stan's offers to help them. This clean-shaven man with the neatly combed hair just didn't seem like the Stan they knew. It was his smile that looked most foreign. But then . . . they didn't know. Stan had gathered up all the old scraps . . . and a loving God had forgiven them.

Come, let's talk this over! says the Lord; no matter how deep the stain of your sins, I can take it out and make you as clean as freshly fallen snow.

Even if you are stained as red as crimson, I can make you white as wool!
(Isa. 1:18 LB).

Coffee breaks at my Dad's church were filled with laughter, warm friendship, and people sharing needs. Everyone looked forward to them, except for one secretary. Robin either avoided coffee breaks or sat in the corner, wishing she were somewhere else.

One day I asked Robin to lunch. She acted as if she wanted to say no, but didn't have the nerve. Several months of cultivating a friendship passed before Robin shared her private fears. She had become a secretary because she considered it a "background job" where she could hide. When she attended college, Robin dropped out of any class that required oral reports or discussion.

She had never felt important to her family. Her parents didn't know how to be supportive or loving. School achievements were mocked, insecurities ridiculed, fears played upon. They never even called her by her name . . . just "girl." Isolation was her form of self-protection.

"Robin, God has always given people what they needed to help them.

"When Peter began to sink into the water, Jesus took his hand.

"For the blind man who evidently needed something concrete to believe, Jesus made spittle. He even touched his eyes a second time.

"*You* are just as important to God as any of those people."

Scraps of empty, lonely yesterdays were presented to God at our weekly prayer times. God, by His incredible loving power, recreated Robin's childhood.

Jesus played with her.
He listened to her.
He was proud of her achievements.
He complimented her desire for an education.
He called her by name.
And He freed her to believe in herself.

It didn't happen in a week or two, but gradually the inner healing made a difference in Robin. She joined a singing group at church, became a teacher of a high school girls' Bible study, and was promoted at work because she became such a valuable employee and spiritual ally.

Hurting, broken scraps had been turned into a new security and confidence.

Don't be afraid . . . I have called you by name; you are mine . . .
For I cried to him and he answered me! He freed me from all my fears (Isa.
43:1; Ps. 34:4 LB).

Early one evening, my phone rang. It was Matt. He sounded frightened.

"Glaphré, can you please come over right away? I don't know what's going on, but I'm scared all the time. I'm jumpy—can't sleep—I don't know what to do. I was thinking that maybe this house I'm renting is haunted or something. Will you come pray for my house?"

I prayed in each of the three rooms, then outside the old dilapidated structure. Before I went back inside, I asked God to give me His wisdom and insight in helping Matt.

Matt met me at the back door and asked anxiously, "Do you think that took care of it?"

"No, Matt, I don't. I don't think the house is the problem."

We sat down in the small living room with orange-crate furniture. Matt was a personable college senior. A leader.

"Matt, I think something *inside of you* is frightening you.

"Glaphré, you know this isn't like me! Whatever it is . . . man, I want to take care of it!"

We prayed and asked God to reveal the source to Matt. As we sat quietly waiting, I heard a noise and looked up.

Matt was pale and shaking—shaking so hard his wooden chair was rocking on its uneven legs.

"What is it, Matt?"

"Nothing. Really!" he answered, obviously frightened. "It can't be what I'm thinking. It happened so long ago and I haven't thought of it in years." Matt was so scared his teeth were chattering loudly. "It's something I've never told anyone."

"Matt, look at you," I said. "Whatever is causing this reaction is important—no matter how long ago it happened."

With a quivering voice that was often hard to understand, Matt related the incident. A nightmare—repeated every night when Matt was ten. It was always the same: A dark room . . . a man on the bed . . . Matt chopping the man into pieces with a hatchet . . . the pieces rising off the bed and chasing Matt. Just as they were about to reach him, Matt always woke up.

"Who was the man, Matt?"

"A man my parents knew. . . ." This tall athlete looked away as he told me what had happened. The man had sexually abused Matt.

With God's help and direction, Matt thought of the scene in his nightmare: The dark room. The man on the bed. Matt with a hatchet.

But this time we asked God to be there. As we prayed, God helped Matt see that the reason for the hatchet was Matt's desperate attempt to free himself from the memory of the abuse.

This time, before Matt could let the hatchet fly against the man, there was a knock at the door. It was Jesus. He had a pair of scissors in His hand.

Jesus knelt before Matt and began to cut the bondage. He began at Matt's feet and cut . . . and cut . . . a gentle Healer working in the frightened memory of one of His children. As Jesus' cutting released Matt from the haunting scraps, his sobbing became so intense his entire body shook.

When we finished this special prayer time, Matt imagined the hatchet falling out of his hand. It was no longer needed.

Jesus then touched and healed all the damage created by the bondage to his past. In time, with Jesus' loving arms around him, Matt was able to forgive the offender.

Worn out, Matt slept uninterrupted for the next forty-eight hours. He's a different young man today. Jesus touched the scraps of Matt's terror. He was free.

So if the Son sets you free, you will be free indeed (John 8:36 NIV).

Arise, and go down to the potter's house,
and there I will cause thee to hear my words.
Then I went down to the potter's house, and, behold,
he wrought a work on the wheels.

And the vessel that he made of clay was marred in the hand of the potter:
so he made it again another vessel,
as seemed good to the potter to make it.

Then the word of the Lord came to me, saying,
O house of Israel, cannot I do with you as this potter?
saith the Lord.

Behold, as the clay is in the potter's hand,
so are ye in mine hand.

(Jer. 18:2–6 KJV).

Part 5.

God Makes the Difference In Our Dreams

———————————————————

Released from our box,
Healed of our scraps,
We stand in awe of God's love.

Then
We collect our fantasies
And proceed with our plans.
Being *whole* will make
The difference!

And God waits.

Chapter 15.

Beyond Our Desires

"Anyone who wants to follow Me
must put aside his own desires" (Luke 9:23 LB).

On one of my weekly trips to the clinic, once again I prayed for quick healing and footnoted all my reasons why this was a good idea. As I entered the waiting room, God reminded me of the opportunities He'd given me here to tell people about Him . . . doctors, nurses, technicians, even other patients.

My response was, "But, God, do I have to be a *patient?* Couldn't I just drop in at coffee break and tell them about You? That seems like a totally workable plan to me!"

While I was waiting to see the doctor, I silently reviewed a memory verse:

But seek ye first the kingdom of God, and his righteousness; and all these things shall be added unto you (Matt. 6:33 KJV).

For several months, I'd been attempting to absorb the truth of this Scripture: Seek God *first.* Why do we tend to seek other things first . . . and want God to be added later?

We seek *success* . . .
and want God to endorse our goals.
We seek *acceptance* . . .
and want God to provide the cheering section.

We seek *increased income* . . .
   and want God to be the bonus.
We seek *vindication* . . .
   and want God to take our side.
We seek *happiness* . . .
   and want God's smile of approval.
We seek *health* . . .
   and want God to dispense an instant cure.

As we mature in our relationship with the Lord, our goals change. But we don't realize that our pattern often remains the same!

We seek to be *useful* . . .
   and want God to bless our busy activities.
We seek to be *helpful to others* . . .
   and want God to tag along.
We seek to be *spiritual* . . .
   and want God to applaud.

We tend to *use* God instead of seek Him. We want God to do our bidding more than we want *Him*.

What percentage of our prayers are for our own comfort? To fulfill our fantasies? Where do we ask for God's will? Isn't it usually at the end of a prayer . . . as a closing benediction . . . sometimes almost as an afterthought?

I wonder how this all-wise God of ours feels about being brought in at the conclusion and asked to bless the plan? What a waste to rely on *our* wisdom, when God's wisdom is available!

A man is a fool to trust himself! But those who use God's wisdom are safe (Prov. 28:26 *LB*).

I had discovered there was no easy formula that would guarantee always getting what we want when we pray. But I was learning there is a better way to live—putting aside *our* desires, *our* dreams . . . and seeking God *first*. Then, ultimately what we needed all along is ours. Perhaps not the problem-free life of our fantasies, but rather fulfillment that isn't fragile. Fulfillment that is too secure to be eroded by imperfect circumstances. The fulfillment is added *after* we seek God first.

I longed for my focus to be so fixed on God that everyone around me would see Him . . . not me. The Holy Spirit was faithfully revealing needed changes—often in unexpected areas. God had even shown me how answering people's continued inquiries about the specifics of my rare illness drew their attention away from Him. Attempting to satisfy curiosity can lock focus on the wrong things. The complicated details of my condition were unimportant. What *was* important was the difference God was making in the midst of my illness.

So, with God's counsel, I had resolved never to discuss the details. Conversations no longer fixed on exploring a medical case history. They no longer cemented me in a "sick mold." There was freedom to see God instead. But . . . what else did I have to learn?

I consider everything a loss compared to the surpassing greatness of knowing Christ Jesus my Lord, for whose sake I have lost all things. I consider them rubbish, that I may gain Christ and be found in Him (Phil. 3:7 NIV, emphasis mine).

A lab technician interrupted my thoughts by asking to talk to me. I followed him to the staff lounge.

"I want to tell you something," he said timidly. "Do you remember when I asked you how you could have so much peace when you know your medical prognosis?"

I did. It had been an opportunity to tell Rick about a God who brings peace in the midst of all circumstances.

"Well, I've been watching you all these months," he continued. "I was skeptical . . . I didn't want to accept what you said about God. I've never known anyone who felt that way about

Him. But I've never known anyone who had such peace, either."
Rick concluded, "I want you to know that, for the first time in my
life, I believe in God."

The nurse found me in the staff lounge talking with Rick and
took me to the treatment room. As she prepared everything, she
said, "You know, I told Mom a few weeks ago I had this patient
who had a peace like no one else I've ever known. Glaphré, I've
come to believe in God, but I feel like I want more than that."

There, in the cold, sterile treatment room, we prayed together.

That same day as I was leaving, one of the supervisors stopped
me in the hall. I'd never seen this stiff, brusque woman look so
nervous. "A lot of people come through this clinic," she said.
"The patients are critically ill, and because they're scared and in
pain, they can be extremely difficult to deal with. I've watched
you . . . I've listened to you . . . and I've listened to what the staff
has said about you.

"I've been a cynic all my life," she admitted. "I've never believed there was a God and have stayed away from anyone who
did. But I want you to know, over the months you've been coming
here, I've . . . well . . . for the first time in my life I believe there is
a God." With that, she turned abruptly and walked away, wiping
her eyes.

By the time I got to my car, I was sobbing. *O God, when am I ever
going to learn that I'm in no position to guide my own life? I would have had
me well long ago. Please forgive me for always wanting my own way.
Thank You for knowing that most of all I want to honor You.*

*You know I want to be well, God. My healing would be easy for You.
But help me leave timing and outcome in Your hands. Help me quit trying to
figure out all the answers. Help me trust You.*

There in a parking lot filled with empty cars . . . using the
steering wheel as my altar . . . our tender God helped me see:

Abraham didn't know where he was going,
   but he knew Who was leading.

The pieces won't always fit . . .
I won't always know why some things do or do not happen,
   But I can know my God.
      And, if I seek Him *first*,
      He will always make a difference.

Not by might, nor by power, but by My spirit, says the Lord . . . My power is made perfect in weakness . . . I the Lord, the first, and with the last; I am He (Zech. 4:6 RSV; 2 Cor. 12:9 NIV; Isa. 41:4 RSV).

Chapter 16.

Beyond Our Commitment

"For apart from Me
you can't do a thing" (John 15:5 LB).

I felt well enough one day to take a drive and discovered a small, rippling river tucked away in a cluster of trees. With no one else in sight, I sat on the dirt river bank for my devotions enjoying the shades of green and the distinctive personalities of the trees. My spirit was longing, as never before, to be intimate with God. I read,

Jesus replied, "The son can do nothing by Himself. He does only what He sees the Father doing, and in the same way" (John 5:19 LB).

Making circles in the water with my feet, I thought, *Do I believe that? Or do I believe Jesus' life and ministry were possible because of what He had going for Him—that He was God's Son? Do I really believe His life and ministry were the result of the choices He made . . . because of a chosen dependency?*

I realized for the first time what I had always done with that verse and other similar Scriptures. I responded to them as if they were nice gestures. Pats on God's back. Thoughtful things for a Son to say. But if Jesus' life and ministry were the result of His dependence on the Father . . .

God was trying to show me a deeper level of relationship with Him. Beyond committing my life to God and being filled with His

Holy Spirit ... beyond accepting and obeying His will ... I needed to *depend* on Him. Not only for the nourishment of my soul, but for the very expression of my life.

Live in vital union with Him. Let your roots grow down into Him and draw up nourishment from Him. See that you go on growing in the Lord (Col. 2:6, 7 LB).

God reminded me of the Israelites huddled in tents outside the Promised Land. They had followed Him through the wilderness, but questioned His ability to protect and care for them in this new land (Ps. 106:24).

Was I doing that? Had I settled into a relationship with God that was comfortable for me, but short of where God wanted to lead me?

I had totally committed my life to God long ago. I still meant it. But I felt as if God were pleading with me.

Glaphré, there is more. More of Myself I want to reveal to you. More I want to do in you. The relationship of total dependency on Me wasn't reserved only for Jesus.

Dependency—the follow-up process to complete commitment. The resolve that is renewed with each new moment, each new event, each new need: To abandon all personal dreams and ideas and desires. To know only GOD ... and let Him direct the moment.

When I began elementary school I took on more responsibilities and disciplines than when I was a preschooler. As an adult I accepted more responsibilities, more disciplines than when I was a teen-ager.

It must be the same with spiritual growth. New levels of growth in Christ had to require new disciplines, new responsibilities. A life of dependency—that disciplined pursuit of intimacy with God—would require always consulting with God and never relying on my own ideas or decisions. Digging out God's will. Discovering His mind.

I didn't know. God could be so pokey sometimes! I wondered if you could ever get anything done that way. It sounded like a lot of hard work.

As I listened to the steady splashing of the river against water-smoothed rocks, I flipped the pages of my Bible. Looking down, I read,

But don't begin until you count the cost (Luke 14:28 LB).

I was scared. I sensed this moment was supposed to make a difference in all the other moments of my life. But I was also facing what was . . . for now, for me . . . the biggest risk, the greatest cost. I was so afraid that taking this step of dependency would trap me in a sick body, forever shutting out complete fulfillment. There was this irrational feeling that maybe *I* could force this thing away. I didn't know what *God* would do if I abandoned to Him my desires and claims on my future. And I wasn't sure I wanted to find out. It seemed too big a chance.

Then, words formed so clearly in my heart they were almost audible.

Glaphré, is My love for you enough? Enough to trust Me with the cost?

I wanted to say *yes*. It broke my heart that all I could say was, *I want it to be.*

Through my tears, I looked at the trees along the river—

All sizes and shapes, green with spring life.
The trees were larger where gnarled roots spread toward the river as if searching for nourishment.
There were two trees,
    taller,
        more majestic than the others.

Their branches were wider,
  with thicker coverings
  of luscious green leaves.

My eyes followed the trunks of these two tallest trees down to find their roots totally covered by water. They were the only trees actually growing *in* the river.

It had to be the same with God. The closer I was to Him, the more His power would be realized in my life.

I felt God's heart reaching out:

Glaphré, don't be one of My children who settles for so little, when there is so much. The choice is yours. You decide *if you walk in the middle of the river, or sit here comfortably getting your feet wet.*

Watching the sun play hide-and-seek with the clouds, I thought, *If Jesus needed to be dependent, then I* certainly do. I stood and looked at the beginning of a sunset. Still scared, I said, *Okay, God. I want the 'more' You talked about. I want to become as close to You as I can. Whatever it costs, teach me to be dependent on You.*

Walking back to the car, I was excited about my tomorrows for the first time since my meeting with the staff of doctors five years earlier. I knew I had made a decision that would change my life. Nothing . . . not even being well . . . could make the kind of difference in my life I needed. Only God. I would learn to seek only Him.

I knew it was a crucial decision.
  But I didn't know it was a decision for
  fulfillment.

But blessed is the man who trusts in the Lord and has made the Lord his hope and confidence. He is like a tree planted along a riverbank, with its roots reaching deep into the water—a tree not bothered by the heat nor worried by long months of drought. Its leaves stay green and it goes right on producing all its luscious fruit (Jer. 17:7, 8 LB).

Chapter 17.

Beyond Our Fantasies

When I think of the wisdom and
scope of your plan . . . (Eph. 3:14a LB).

*A*fter a few years of actively pursuing dependency on such unfamiliar paths as the year of travel, I began to feel that God wanted me to give my life to prayer . . . whatever that meant!

This time it wasn't like the school or the travel assignment. For even though I didn't understand what it was all about, I didn't resist God's direction. I just needed to be sure it was what God wanted. After three months of seeking, I was sure.

"I'm not clear about what you're going to be doing now. Exactly what is it?" asked friends and fellow church members.

Responding with great spiritual insight, I'd answer, "I don't know."

And I didn't. I had visions of living the life of a monk . . . cloistered in my apartment . . . never seeing the light of day again. I only knew I was to give my life to prayer, and trust God for my livelihood. I didn't know what would be required of me, but how wonderful to be completely at peace in the face of not knowing. Me . . . who likes to have an orderly plan for everything . . . now able to be comfortable beginning an unknown journey.

I knew only two things: I was to be available to pray for and with people; I was never to share my financial needs with anyone, not even with my family.

I spent my time eagerly learning more about prayer. Learning as the Holy Spirit interpreted my great Friend, the Word of God. And what a privilege to pray for others.

God was creating a dream.

"We'd like you to hold a seminar on prayer for us," requested my church staff. I'd never even thought of such a thing. After I prayed about it, I asked if I could develop completely different seminars for adults, teens, and children. The staff agreed.

I asked the church secretaries to make forty copies of the adult material. Since I knew that most people considered praying ineffective and tedious, forty seemed a generous projection.

We were not prepared for the response: 150 adults came the first night; over 300, the second night; and almost 600, the third night. We changed rooms twice. I was in shock. I knew there was a need; I just didn't know there was an interest.

Other churches began requesting prayer seminars, and the number of people asking for prayer counseling appointments grew. More and more they were people I didn't know. Often they needed healing of scraps, freedom from boxes. Sometimes they needed physical healing.

God, my praying for people's healing is crazy! Why would anyone want me—someone who is sick—to pray for healing?

But God graciously allows me to be around while *He* ministers. It's easy to trust others to a God I know to be loving.

Eventually Prayerlife®, a nonprofit organization, was formed. The approach remained the same: God was to direct all our activities; we were never to solicit money, or even share financial needs. God also had personal guidelines for me: I could only teach those things that had been proven in my own experience, and no more than half my time could be given to holding seminars. The rest of my time was to be spent in a personal prayer ministry and learning about prayer from God. I had no right to teach if I were not growing myself.

Although I enjoyed all the jobs I held as an adult, none of them matched the fulfillment of writing the seminars and notebooks on prayer. What a joy to receive God's direction on what children and teens and adults needed to learn and unlearn about prayer. And God reminded me of instances where He'd proven those truths in my own life.

God had been preparing me for His dream.

After I had written the notebooks for the adult seminar, I learned that the initial printing costs totaled $1,000. I waited. While in Florida, I received a long-distance phone call from a couple in Oklahoma, who felt impressed to give $1,000 to Prayerlife.

One thousand dollars! I could hardly believe it. That was so much more than I'd ever received before. And without anyone at all knowing the need, the exact amount had been given. I ordered the first small shipment of notebooks.

Praying for people was a great privilege. But helping them learn to turn to God for help . . . that was a dream I'd never dared to have.

One day my doorbell rang. It was a friend with a big bowl of fruit. I thanked her for her thoughtfulness, never hinting I was completely out of money and food. I thanked God for the fruit as I washed it and put it away. Then . . . hidden inside I discovered a hundred-dollar bill. God has always been faithful.

More and more I longed for people to know God's love.
To know His eagerness to communicate with them.
To know God's commitment to make a difference—
to *be* the difference in their lives.

The dream was taking shape.

As I grew physically weaker, the dream grew stronger. I wrote a few friends, asking them to consider praying regularly for Prayerlife with me. These friends have become prayer partners with whom I share my schedule and areas of need, different groups of prayer partners for each seminar: Adults pray for the adult and family seminars; teens, for the teen seminar; and children, for their seminar. As the seminars ministered, people I had never met wrote me offering their prayer support. Over three hundred prayer partners now regularly pray for this ministry. Their investment of faith and prayer is a major part of all God does through Prayerlife.

Eventually, I was no longer physically able to hold the seminars, and I began praying for God's protection of His message. I thought a pretty good way to do that would be to make me well. (Yes, I still give God suggestions!)

Then . . . the idea of putting all the seminars on videotape. I wanted to run from it. I didn't know anything about videotape, and I didn't *want* to know anything about it.

The idea grew stronger, so I did some investigation. *Beginning* the project would take $10,000! It was easy to present a fifty-dollar need to God . . . but $10,000 . . . that was ridiculous!

Finally, I stopped avoiding God and prayed, *God, if this is You instead of some wild idea I've dreamed up on my own, I ask for a significant witness of your Spirit* this week. *I don't want this to drag out any longer.*

At the end of the week, a man I had never met received a letter from one of his friends telling of the help received from "Glaphré's seminars." The same day he got the letter, this man, who didn't even know that "Glaphré" was the name of a person, gave $10,000 to Prayerlife.

Okay! Okay, God! I guess we can count this as a fairly significant sign that You want the seminars on videotape.

There's a difference between fantasies and dreams.

Fantasies carry no responsibilities.
Dreams demand more responsibility
than can be fulfilled without God.
Fantasies avoid reality.
Dreams look reality in the face and say,
"God, what do we do about this?"

When the videotape project needed more money, I sold the small house Dad had helped me buy, even before I moved into it.

The same friends who had given me the Bibles for my birthday the year I traveled, offered me their guest quarters.

Although people miraculously gave at the moment of need, soon the project was in need of money again. I sold my car. (Not the broken-down one, but a really special white Volkswagen that actually ran.) Lin, my sister-in-law, and Robin, the secretary at the church, shared their cars with me.

Selling the house and car were not hard decisions to make. There was no struggle here. God was developing the dream, and it was a joy to be part of it.

My personal physician, who has always encouraged my ministry, contributed an old house to Prayerlife. His intention was to provide a storage area for our materials. Although my hosts had been gracious about my extended stay in their guest room, I decided I'd live in the Prayerlife house. My doctor looked shocked when I told him. "I'll . . . uh . . . need to . . . uh . . . fix it up."

"Absolutely not. Your gift has already been extremely generous," I insisted.

Uncharacteristically Dad's voice choked back tears when I told him I was going to move into the house. "I can't handle your living there, Glaphré. It's not livable, and you're too weak to battle the heat."

"It's going to be okay, Dad." My reassurances were partly in faith, partly out of ignorance. I had no idea what kind of work the house needed. I didn't know the plumbing needed a total overhaul. That none of the bathroom fixtures worked. That most of the electrical wiring needed reworking. I *had* noticed that layers of wallpaper and paint were peeling off.

A phone call. "Glaphré, my wife and I were really helped by your seminar a couple of years ago. We'd like to install central air and heat in your house as a gift."

I cried. Their gift would definitely make a difference in my ability to function.

The caller didn't stop there. He also put in hookups for a

washer-dryer. His son reworked all the plumbing. His friends replastered the ceiling and rewired the electricity.

Twenty junior-highers from church worked on the lawn for a string of Saturdays. The former members of the college Sunday school class I used to teach, now young adults, spearheaded work crews of thirty and more to scrape the many coats of paint and wallpaper before repainting.

"Hi!"

I looked up from my attempt at helping the paint crew and saw a stranger in the doorway. "I hear lots of neat things happen to people who work on this house. One guy got some property he'd wanted for several years. Another guy couldn't afford a truck he needed for his work, but after he did some carpentry work on this house, one turned up at his price. Stuff like that. Can I work on the house?"

Every time I went over to check on the house, there were new surprises. Carpet. Insulation. Shrubbery. Light fixtures. A bathtub. A pantry. Wallpaper. Curtains. Window blinds. A washer-dryer. A fence. Everyone doing his own thing. And it all went together beautifully. (God is even a good interior decorator!)

I've never had a desire to live in a new house; I always wanted to live in an old one. And here I was! My lovely home even had a room arrangement that was perfect for my needs. The back part of the house, with one of the two bedrooms serving as my living room, is my residence. The living room and connecting garage form our office. The house is located in a business district on Highway 66, a perfect location for the office.

And Jesus replied, "Let me assure you that no one has ever given up anything—home, brothers, sisters, mother, father, children, or property— for love of Me and to tell others the Good News, who won't be given back, a hundred times over (Mark 10:29, 30a LB).

As the dream developed, I learned more about God's ability to guide in the face of absolute ignorance. After we finished taping, I didn't know anyone to go to for supervision in the editing of the tapes. I needed a miracle!

The phone rang. "Glaphré, I'm a film and television producer here in Hollywood. I attended a Prayerlife seminar last year and it helped me so much that I want to give something back. I'd like to offer my services to supervise the editing of your videotapes as a gift."

Bryan made a tremendous difference in the quality of our videotapes. His skills. His contacts. His enthusiasm. He and God even taught me how to edit. Being a basic have-trouble-operating-an-electric-can-opener type person, my learning to edit seemed no less a miracle than the parting of the Red Sea.

Companies in Hollywood gave discounts and offered us free services. One company even took a loss to help us, absorbing their own cost. I thanked Bryan for opening doors and making arrangements. "It's not me. You don't understand. This kind of thing just doesn't happen in Hollywood. It just doesn't happen!"

But it did! God had made the difference.

My family and friends have encouraged me, believed in the dream, and given many hours of volunteer work. My family has sacrificed to help the dream become a reality.

The dream is tailor-made for me. It even helps fulfill my deep love for children by allowing me to teach them about a God who loves them. What a fun dream!

There aren't many dreams that could be continued when you are confined to bed most of the time. But, you see, this dream is from God to me, and circumstances don't control it . . . God does.

People are so kind to write about God's ministry to them through Prayerlife. The letters that often mean the most are from those who attended years before, for they speak of a *lasting* difference:

From an elderly man: "When I attended the Prayerlife Seminar a year-and-a-half ago, I hadn't been in church for twenty years. For the first time, I felt God's presence and I've been attending church ever since."

From a child: "Prayerlife helped me when my parents were getting a divorce. It helped me not fight about things because I was mad."

From Idaho: "The Prayerlife Seminar came just in time to save my marriage and my self-concept. God used it to heal my hurts. Thank you."

From a teen: "I never knew how much God loved me before."

From a deputy warden of a federal prison: "Your videotape seminars have met the most basic needs of our men. The men left the seminar believing that no matter how rotten things were, they could still have a relationship with Jesus."

From Swaziland: "My doctor-husband and I are spending some time here in Swaziland, where I recently attended a Prayerlife Seminar. During the seminar, I accepted Jesus as my Savior. It's a new beginning for me!"

From a middle-aged man: "I've never heard of anyone being healed watching a videotape. But I was! Praise God!"

An anonymous note: "One year—a year I thought I'd always have to live with—is forgiven. Now I can face all the years ahead. Thank you!"

From a father: "Thank you for what you taught my son on prayer via videotape . . ." His letter described a poignant story:

A Christian family. A troubled teen-aged daughter. Suffocating tension and piercing clash of wills resulted in the daughter leaving home. Days passed. Weeks passed. Months passed. And there was no contact with her.

The quiet of hopeless desperation filled the house. The remorse of not being all-wise, of not having all the answers haunted the parents.

A phone call. The daughter wanted to come home.

Amid the tears and hugging and joy, the seven-year-old son exclaimed, "Daddy, it's an answer to prayer."

Startled, the father knelt down before this miniature reflection of himself. "What do you mean, son?"

"At Prayerlife, I learned God can help us with anything. Ever since, I've prayed every day that Stacey would call."

"But, that's been almost two months." The dad questioned a seven-year-old's ability to pray that long about anything.

"I know, Daddy," the son responded. "You have to keep praying till you get all the help you need. It's an answer to prayer!"

The dad wrapped his long arms all the way around his son, and silently prayed, "God, all this time . . . and it's never even occurred to me to pray that Stacey would call. Thank you for teaching my son to pray."

Don't let anyone think little of you because you are young . . . be a pattern for them (1 Tim. 4:12 LB).

From a minister: "So many of our church families were affected in such a profound way by the Prayerlife Seminar, but little did I realize my own family would receive the greatest benefit . . ."

A lovely young woman, too shy to be the pastor's wife she wanted to be. Through the seminar, God touched her feelings about herself. She walked into her responsibilities, freed to minister and secure enough to enjoy it. But, much more than that. Released from cautious self-doubt, Kay actively pursued increased fellowship with her God.

"Exactly one year after the seminar, I was told the shocking news that my thirty-three-year-old wife had lung cancer," writes the minister-husband. "Our dreams were so young and exciting . . . Lisa, our three-year-old daughter needed her mother so much, and I could not imagine my own life without Kay as my wife. But less than two months later, the doctor's words were fulfilled—Kay died.

"How did Prayerlife affect us? For the previous twelve months, Kay had used her Prayerlife notebook as a devotional aid. Through prayer, Kay came to know her Heavenly Father as *Father*.

"Through the painful ordeal of surgery, chemotherapy, radiation treatments, and endless tests . . . friends who came to encourage Kay were, instead, encouraged by her. They came to love in a time of death, and left with a challenge to live. . . . Through it all, Kay's life was characterized by peace—indescribable peace.

"During the last months of her life, Kay's most important possession, apart from her personal Bible, was her Prayerlife notebook. It is much like a diary, and it gives such a beautiful description of her spiritual journey from the Prayerlife Seminar in April, 1978, to the front door of her Father's home in June, 1979.

"Glaphré, through prayer I have come to know God as a God of integrity and love. I can build my life on that."

Sincerely in Christ,
Mark M. Goodwin
Pastor

"I am leaving you with a gift—peace of mind and heart! And the peace isn't fragile . . . so don't be afraid." (John 14: 27 LB).

The calling . . . to seek God.
The dream . . . to help others discover
intimate fellowship with God.
  I gave God my fantasies.
  He gave me His Dream.

Now glory be to God who by His mighty power at work within us is able to do far more than we would ever dare to ask or even dream of—infinitely beyond our highest prayers, desires, thoughts, or hopes (Eph. 3:20 LB).

They refused to enter the Promised Land,
for they wouldn't believe His solemn oath to care for them.
Instead, they pouted in their tents.

Trust wholeheartedly in Yahweh, put no faith in your own perception.

I am the vine; you are the branches . . .
apart from Me you can do nothing.

When I call Thee to mind upon my bed and think on Thee
in the watches of the night, remembering how
Thou has been my help and that I am safe
in the shadow of Thy wings,
then I humbly follow Thee with all my heart.

Into your hands I commit my spirit . . .
I shall be satisfied when I awake with thy likeness.

(Ps. 106:24, 25 LB; Prov. 3:5 JB; John 15:5 NIV; Ps. 63:6–8 NEB; Luke 23:46 NIV; Ps. 17:15 KJV).

Part 6.

God Makes the Difference In Our Hope

WHATEVER YOUR CIRCUMSTANCES, WHATEVER YOUR SCRAPS,

GOD CAN MAKE THE DIFFERENCE!

I KNOW.
BECAUSE HE DID FOR ME.

Chapter 18.

God Has a Dream for You

Choose to love the Lord your
God and to obey Him and to cling
to Him for He is your life and the
length of your days (Deut. 30:20 LB).

I'm one of God's slow learners. Sometimes I cry out, *God, don't
look at me. I'm so far from what I should be!*

Then a gentle and loving God reminds me,

Look at Me *and discover the 'more' I have for you.*

God makes a difference. He changes my focus.

I have struggled with showing you my box of self-imposed
limitations, for your hurt may be so much greater. Your circumstances, so much more difficult.

Then a present and all-wise God reminds me,

No matter how the cause or degree of your hurts may differ, I am *the same.
I am as powerful, as willing to touch and free and heal.* I am able to
make the difference.

I didn't want to expose my scraps yet. I wanted to wait until I
could tell you, "I'm totally well. I feel good! I no longer have to
spend most of my time in bed!" (Being a former teacher, I keep

141

giving God a multiple choice of how and when to heal me. So far, He keeps writing in "none of the above.") Maybe someday I can say that to you. But not now.

Then, God reminds me. I *can* tell you this:

I'm healed *inside*.
Inside I'm whole.
The scraps are gone.

Maybe it's important for you to know that my circumstances haven't changed. But *I* have. You see, I know! I really know!

What I become doesn't have to be determined
by what I feel like
or look like
or can't do.
What I become can be determined
by what I allow God to be
in me.
God makes the difference.

That's why I can say . . .
To my friend, Rich,
who at thirty became a quadriplegic because of a
car accident.
To Fran,
who, shattered by an abusive mate, is afraid to hope
for any kind of happiness.
To Bill,
who became a Christian in mid-life, and is haunted
by the lost years.
To Merl and Kay,
whose feeling of failure over a troubled child
chokes their potential.
To Marlene,
who is alone.

To Ray,
  who thinks all meaningful doors to the future are
  closed, and doesn't know why.

It's not perfected circumstances,
  or a perfected self.
It's the perfectness of our God
  and His commitment to us
  that brings beauty to life.

Don't make the mistake I did. Don't make life and God com-
pete with your fantasies of a utopia without problems. Don't
believe the spiritual hype we're often handed today that says if
you only "believe," all your problems will disappear. The words
of Jesus belie that false doctrine.

How much of your life is passing while you wait for those
perfected circumstances? How many weeks . . . and months . . .
and years?

Our sovereign God *does* release His power in our situations.
Believe God for miraculous changes in your circumstances. But in the
meantime, *there can be miraculous changes in you.* It's been twelve
years since I gave God my scraps. I can tell you . . . the difference
lasts.

Your calling is to seek God. Your dream will be how God
chooses to interpret that calling through *you.* God's dream for you
may not bring a vocational change, yet it may bring a directional
change.

Real estate agents: As God directs, you could share with your
clients the One who makes a house a home.

Baby-sitters: You could pray for your charges and involve them
in projects of kindness.

Delivery men: You could pray for your customers. You could
ask God to show them the Deliverer through you.

Coaches: You could pray for your team, asking God to teach
them the most important victory in life.

Husbands and wives: You could rely not only on books, instincts, or the world's trends to know what kind of mate you should be. You could seek God's counsel in your marriage.

Parents: You could believe in your children's need to know God's love. In your teen's spiritual potential. Be your children's faithful prayer support, whatever their age.

I don't know what God's dream is for you. But if you look at your life and see . . .

> scraps of the past that rob you of fulfillment,
> scraps that capture loneliness and won't let it go,
> scraps that bind off hope's circulation,

I long for you to know . . .
There is a God.
    He accepts boxes.
      He heals scraps.
        He forgives.
          He has a dream with your name on it.
God makes the difference. I know He can do it for you. You see, He did for me.

With the Peace and Joy
of Belonging to God,

Glaphré

All this will be because the mercy of our God is very tender, and heaven's dawn is about to break upon us, to give light to those who sit in darkness and death's shadow, and to guide us to the path of peace (Luke 1:78, 79 LB).